PREACHING
SECOND CORINTHIANS

PROCLAMATION:
Preaching the New Testament

Before the rise of historical criticism as the dominant mode of interpretation in the eighteenth century, biblical commentaries were written for the church with homiletical interests in mind. Since the Enlightenment, the critical commentary has largely excluded ecclesiastical and homiletical interests. In introducing the Meyer series in 1831, H. A. W. Meyer set the standard for subsequent commentaries, indicating that this commentary would exclude philosophical and ecclesiastical concerns and would concentrate on what the original authors meant in their own historical context.

This standard creates a challenge for preachers whose task is to bring a living word to listeners, most of whom do not come to church out of antiquarian interests. Some commentaries have attempted to overcome the gap between the historical interests of the critical commentary and the homiletical concerns of the preacher by publishing parallel sections—one providing critical scholarship and the other offering guidance for preaching.

While biblical scholars specialize in a specific genre or book of Scripture, preachers are responsible for interpreting the entire canon over an extended time. As commentaries are increasingly complex, few preachers have the opportunity to mine the information and reflect an awareness of contemporary scholarship on each passage. Thus they face the challenge of merging the horizons between critical scholarship and a living word for the congregation.

In these volumes, scholar-preachers and preacher-scholars offer a guide for preachers, bringing the horizons of past and present together. The series is not a typical commentary, but a guide for preachers that offers the results of scholarship for the sake of preaching. Writers in this series will reflect an awareness of critical scholarship but will not focus on the details involved in a commentary. Rather, they will offer the fruits of critical scholarship reflected in explanations of sections of the biblical text. After a brief discussion of the major issues in a book—the central issues—each volume will be arranged by sections with an eye to what is useful for the sermon.

Authors in the Proclamation series will describe the major focus of each section, recognizing the place of the passage in the context of the book. Authors will look to the rhetorical impact of the text, asking "what does the text do?" Does it reassure the hearers? Does it lead them in worship and praise? Does it indict? Does it encourage? The Proclamation series will guide preachers in recognizing the essential rhetorical focus of the passage towards representing the impact of the text for today.

While preachers offer a living word for a specific situation, they also speak to larger cultural issues that face every congregation. Consequently, writers in this series may employ their knowledge of the ancient situation to suggest how the ancient word speaks across the centuries to parallel situations in our own time.

Accompanying the discussion writers may employ sermons, outlines, or other resources that further empower today's preachers in making the use of scholarship for the good of the church today.

Series Editors:

James W. Thompson is Scholar in Residence at the Graduate School of Theology as well as the editor for Restoration Quarterly.

Jason A. Myers is Associate Professor of Biblical Studies at Greensboro College, Greensboro, NC.

Preaching
SECOND CORINTHIANS

James W. Thompson

CASCADE *Books* · Eugene, Oregon

PREACHING SECOND CORINTHIANS

Proclamation: Preaching the New Testament

Cascade Books
An Imprint of Wipf and Stock Publishers
199 W. 8th Ave., Suite 3
Eugene, OR 97401

www.wipfandstock.com

PAPERBACK ISBN: 978-1-7252-5834-1
HARDCOVER ISBN: 978-1-7252-5835-8
EBOOK ISBN: 978-1-7252-5836-5

Cataloguing-in-Publication data:

Names: Thompson, James W., author.

Title: Preaching Second Corinthians / by James W. Thompson.

Description: Eugene, OR: Cascade Books, 2021 | Series: Proclamation: Preaching the New Testament | Includes bibliographical references.

Identifiers: ISBN 978-1-7252-5834-1 (paperback) | ISBN 978-1-7252-5835-8 (hardcover) | ISBN 978-1-7252-5836-5 (ebook)

Subjects: LCSH: Bible. Corinthians, 2nd—Criticism, interpretation, etc. | Bible. Corinthians, 2nd—Sermons | Preaching—Biblical teaching.

Classification: BS2655.P8 T56 2021 (print) | BS2655.P8 (ebook)

Manufactured in the U.S.A.   February 1, 2021

CONTENTS

INTRODUCTION

Preaching in the Midst of Competing Voices

DESPITE PAUL'S CONCESSION IN 2 Corinthians that he is "untrained in speech" (11:6) and his opposition's charge that "his speech is contemptible" (2 Cor 10:10), no epistle exhibits more rhetorical power than this one. Preachers may discover inviting preaching texts in the numerous memorable phrases of the letter that have become popular slogans. This rhetorical power is often evident in the brilliant metaphors of the letter. Paul's exclamation "But thanks be to God who always leads us in a triumphal procession" (2:14) and his declaration "We are the aroma of Christ" (2:15) provide metaphors that resonate for preaching. Similarly, his claim that "we hold this treasure in clay jars" (4:7) provides another striking metaphor for the preacher. In other passages, Paul speaks with an epigrammatic style that grasps the imagination of the preacher and congregation. Such phrases as "the letter kills, but the Spirit gives life" (2 Cor 3:6), "if anyone is in Christ, there is a new creation" (5:17), and "whenever I am weak, then I am strong" (12:10) reflect the rhetorical power of the letter. Similarly, Paul summarizes the Christian faith in the statements "For you know the generous act of our Lord Jesus Christ, that though he was rich, yet for your sakes he became poor" (8:9) and "God was in Christ reconciling the world to himself" (2 Cor 5:19).

Such striking phrases, as inviting as they may be for preachers, may be seductively simple, enticing us to separate them from their context in 2 Corinthians. What appear, at first glance, to be slogans suitable for bumper stickers actually belong to a heated discussion between Paul and the Corinthians involving issues that have confronted the church from Paul's time until now. In order to preach these passages faithfully, we must recognize

1

their place in an ancient conversation between Paul and the Corinthians—the longest recorded conversation of Paul with his churches.

Paul and the Corinthians: A Lengthy Conversation

Second Corinthians is the last recorded stage in a conversation that began at least five years earlier, when Paul founded this church. The details of Paul's relationship with the Corinthians are available in the major commentaries. Here we note that Paul established the Corinthian congregation in the bustling new city of Corinth, which had been rebuilt on the ruins of the old city that had been destroyed by Julius Caesar in 146 BCE, approximately a century before Paul's arrival. The Corinthian church apparently reflected the diversity of the new city of Corinth, which had been repopulated by Jews, Greeks, Romans, and immigrants from throughout the Roman world. The church also reflected the socioeconomic range of the new city, for it included among its members both poor people and a minority of members who shared the new wealth of Corinth as well as the social pretensions that accompanied that wealth (cf. 1 Cor 1:26–28).

Paul began his task of building a church on his initial visit, most likely in 49 CE. During this time he baptized many Corinthians and then remained with the community for eighteen months (Acts 18:11). The evidence of 1 Corinthians suggests that Paul taught the new converts the traditions that were meant to provide a shared congregational culture (1 Cor 11:2, 23–26; 15:3–5). Because Paul knew that this extended period was not adequate to develop the Corinthians into a body, after his departure he wrote the Corinthians a letter (1 Cor 5:9), no longer extant, urging them not to associate with immoral people.

By the time Paul wrote 1 Corinthians, the conversation had gone further. His original letter needed clarification. The Corinthians evidently asked if his prohibition of association with immoral people extended even to unbelievers (1 Cor 5:9–11). Paul heard reports from Chloe's people (1 Cor 1:10–11) that the Corinthians were divided into factions. He also received reports from the household of Stephanas (1 Cor 16:15–18). In addition, the Corinthians had written a letter to Paul requesting further instruction on a variety of issues (1 Cor 7:1; 8:1; 12:1).

The issues Paul faced reflect the extraordinary challenge of building a community of faith among new believers, who have brought their own cultural values into the community. Although the Corinthians had originally accepted Paul's message of the crucified and risen savior (1 Cor 1:18–25; 15:3), the controversies that erupted after Paul left Corinth suggest that the new converts did not grasp the implications of that message. The socially pretentious among the Corinthians were exercising an influence that extended beyond their numbers (cf. 1 Cor 1:26–28). Paul's refusal to accept them as patrons and his insistence on working with his hands (1 Cor 4:9–12) became a source of enmity among some of the wealthy members.[1] In a culture that associated wisdom with rhetorical ability and accorded to orators the status that only rock stars and world-class athletes enjoy today, Paul evidently did not measure up to Apollos or the orators of the time. The Corinthians brought their secular values into the church, demonstrating the same partisan spirit that often existed among orators and their students. They claimed to be wise (3:18) and to possess personal freedom. With their slogan that "all things are lawful" (1 Cor 6:12; 10:23), they insisted on their own rights, even if their exercise of individual freedom undermined the faith of others within the community. Factions were also present in the community's worship (chs. 12–14), where anti-communal tendencies threatened the unity of the church. In the Lord's Supper, the divisions between rich and poor were especially evident, for wealthy Christians treated the Lord's Supper as if it were a Hellenistic meal. Their claim that "there is no resurrection of the dead" (1 Cor 15:12) also reflects the continuing presence of the belief system that they held prior to their conversion.

In 1 Corinthians Paul responds to the crisis, attempting to do what he had not been able to do during his eighteen months in Corinth: to reorient the minds of the Corinthians from the values of their previous existence to a new mindset shaped by the cross (chs. 1–4). The partisan behavior in Corinth, according to Paul, is a sign that many Corinthians are behaving in a secular way—of behaving as "according to human inclinations" (1 Cor 3:3).[2] When the Corinthians recognize the significance of the word of the cross—a message they had all believed at the beginning—they will abandon the selfish exercise of freedom that undermines community and recognize the importance of not exercising one's rights for the sake of "the one for whom Christ died" (1 Cor 8:9). Those who understand the message of the cross will forego taking a brother to court (1 Cor 6:1–11), visiting the prostitute (1 Cor 6:12–20), and insisting on their rights to eat food offered to idols (8:1—11:1). In their worship service, they will demonstrate

1. Marshall, *Enmity at Corinth*, 15–18, 173–81.
2. Winter, *After Paul Left Corinth*, 40.

concern for the poor at the Lord's Supper (1 Cor 11:17–34) and exercise their own gifts for the sake of the community (1 Cor 14:1–5). Corinthians who recall what they confessed originally (1 Cor 15:3–5, 12) will no longer question the resurrection of believers as they did in their earlier existence but will celebrate God's victory in Jesus Christ.

At the conclusion of 1 Corinthians, Paul promises to continue the conversation with the community on his next journey (1 Cor 16:5–8). He sends the letter with Timothy, whom Paul commissions to explain his ways (1 Cor 4:17; 16:10). The evidence from 2 Corinthians suggests that Timothy finds even more problems during his visit to Corinth. Timothy's report results in the "painful visit" (2 Cor 2:1), in which Paul faces open rebellion from some of the Corinthians (cf. 2:5–11). He returns and writes a letter "with many tears" (2:4), attempting to correct the situation in Corinth. He sends the letter by Titus, hoping to meet him later in Troas (2:12–13) and to receive a report on the Corinthian situation. When Paul finally encounters Titus in Macedonia, he receives a favorable report about the Corinthians. Titus reports that the Corinthians have repented of their open rebellion and that they desire to see Paul again (7:5–16). Titus brings the news that Paul's severe letter has brought the desired results, and Paul expresses relief and satisfaction at the congregation's change of heart.

Paul's interaction with the Corinthians reveals both the anguish and joy of his pastoral ministry. Indeed, the puzzling feature of 2 Corinthians is that expressions of joy, anguish, desperation, and bitterness exist within the same letter. The alternation of tone and the sudden shift of subject matter at several places in the letter present a challenge to the reader. For example, in 7:5–16 Paul places his anguish over the Corinthians in the past tense (2:12–13; 7:5), describing how Titus's arrival turned his restless spirit into joy at the progress of the Corinthians. However, chapters 10–13 are distinguished by a threatening tone and bitter sarcasm (cf. 11:20–21) as Paul anticipates a third visit (cf. 2:3) to them. He writes the letter, indicating that he hopes not to act severely on this next visit (13:10). A similar change in subject matter occurs in chapters 1–7. The narrative of recent events that culminated with Paul's relief at the coming of Titus (7:5–16) is a continuous story that began in 1:1—2:13 with an account of the events that occurred after the writing of 2 Corinthians. Paul's statement in 2:13, "My mind could not rest because I did not find my brother Titus there," is not continued until 7:5–6, when he says, "For even when we came into Macedonia, our bodies had no rest, . . . but God consoled us by the arrival of Titus." Between this continuous narrative of past events is a defense of Paul's current ministry in 2:14—7:4 in the present tense. The latter passage exhibits another of the puzzling digressions when Paul's appeal to the Corinthians "not to be unequally yoked to unbelievers" (6:14—7:1), a theme mentioned nowhere else in 2 Corinthians, is sandwiched between his appeals to "Open wide your hearts also" (6:13) and "Make room in your hearts for us" (7:2).

Most scholars attempt to resolve the problems posed by 2 Corinthians by suggesting that the letter is a composite of letters to Corinth reflecting more than one stage in Paul's conversation with the Corinthians. The major commentaries provide the alternative reconstructions. Some suggest that the bitter tone of chapters 10–13 reflects an earlier stage in Paul's relationship to the Corinthians than that in chapters 1–9. A view held by many scholars is that chapters 10–13 include at least a portion of the "tearful letter" mentioned in 2:2. Others suggest that chapters 10–13 reflect a stage in Paul's relationship with the Corinthians after he wrote chapters 1–9 and received new information. I suggest, however, that attempts to reconstruct separate letter fragments and to determine their sequence create as many problems for the reader as they solve. An increasing number of scholars, recognizing that the letters are actually speeches that Paul dictated, observe that the sudden changes of tone and the repetition that one finds in 2 Corinthians were not uncommon in the oral culture of antiquity.[3] Some scholars have noted, for example, that Demosthenes, *Epistle* 2, is closely parallel with 2 Corinthians insofar as Demosthenes writes to the people of Athens to defend himself against accusations and to plead for his restoration.[4] The striking thing about his speech is that he begins by commending the Athenians and treating his position as an exception to their usual scrupulous attention to evidence and fairness in judgment. He goes on to speak of his own services to the city and to Greece in general—though with hesitation. He reviews the events that led to the present situation and enumerates points in his favor. He then answers the points against him. Finally, he sums up his plea in far more passionate terms than he has dared to use earlier in the letter, appealing to the Athenians to save him. Demosthenes's defense conforms to the forensic speech and is parallel in many respects to 2 Corinthians.[5]

---

3. Long, *Ancient Rhetoric and Paul's Apology*; Amador, "Revisiting 2 Corinthians"; Witherington, *Conflict and Community in Corinth*.

4. See also Danker, "Paul's Debt to the *De Corona* of Demosthenes," 268.

5. See Young and Ford, *Meaning and Truth in 2 Corinthians*, 37.

Our preaching from 2 Corinthians does not depend on any single partition theory, for several factors suggest that one may approach the entirety of 2 Corinthians as one letter and analyze the rhetorical impact of the entire work. Like other Pauline letters, it opens with a thanksgiving and concludes with Paul's future travel plans (12:14–18; 13:1–3) and a benediction (13:13). Despite the sudden shifts in tone, the subject remains the same throughout the letter. Paul defends himself to his own community in response to the charges against his ministry. The topic of the ministry (*diakonia*) and the minister (*diakonos*) is at the center of the discussion in both 1–9 and 10–13. Indeed, the term *diakonos* (or *diakonia*) appears more in 2 Corinthians than in all of the other undisputed letters of Paul combined (2 Cor 3:3, 6–10; 4:1; 5:18; 6:3–4; 8:4; 9:1, 12; 11:8, 15, 23). Paul is on the defensive throughout the letter, answering charges that he is not a true *diakonos*.

Paul's defense of his ministry in 2 Corinthians is a continuation of the conversation with this troublesome church and a reminder that Paul's pastoral ministry, like most ministries after his, proceeded from one crisis to another and that the formation of a church is an unfinished task. In 2 Corinthians we discover old issues from 1 Corinthians that have not been resolved and new issues that call for Paul's response. The evidence of 2 Corinthians suggests that sometime after Paul wrote 1 Corinthians, missionaries came to Corinth and allied themselves with those who had opposed Paul in 1 Corinthians. Paul finds himself in a triangular relationship involving himself, the Corinthian church, and "some" (2:17; 3:1; 10:2) who have influenced the Corinthians against Paul. Consequently, Paul's rhetorical ability and his refusal to accept financial support for his work continue to be issues in 2 Corinthians (10:1, 10–11; 11:7). In addition, new issues emerge in 2 Corinthians. The opponents of 2 Corinthians claim to be "ministers of Christ" (11:23) and apostles (11:6, 13), whom Paul describes as "false apostles" (11:13) and "super apostles" (11:5). They supply their own letters of recommendation (3:1), which commend them with boasts of their achievements. They compare themselves with Paul (10:12) and force him to offer his own ministerial and apostolic credentials. The opponents have criticized Paul's credentials, claiming that his weak physical presence (10:11), lack of rhetorical ability (11:6), humility (10:1; 11:7), and weakness (cf. 11:21) are indications that Paul is not a man of the Spirit (10:3). We may assume that the opponents claim for themselves the qualities of boldness, strength, and physical presence that they do not find in Paul. In addition, the opponents are not hesitant to demand financial support (2:17) or to make demands on the Corinthians (cf. 11:16–21). In ridiculing Paul's humility, the opponents have portrayed him in terms of the stock figure of the flatterer, a well-known designation in antiquity. Flatterers are false friends who tell their listeners what they want to hear in order to gain favor. They are always servile and humble people, debasing themselves for their own advantage.[6]

Against these criticisms, Paul reluctantly "commends himself" to the Corinthians (4:2; 6:4) and even boasts of his achievements throughout the letter. The epistle is the most autobiographical of Paul's letters because he has been forced into professional boasting. From beginning to end, Paul defends his ministry to the congregation that he founded. The periodic refrain in 2 Corinthians is the catalog of sufferings (*peristasis* catalog) that lists Paul's experiences as a minister (4:7–11; 6:4–10; 11:23–33). He describes this catalog of sufferings as a foolish exercise in boasting forced on him by the Corinthians (12:11). The list of sufferings is, however, filled with irony. Unlike the opponents who list the obstacles that they have overcome as evidence of their power, Paul actually lists the experiences that demonstrate his weakness (11:30).

The issue of 2 Corinthians is the legitimacy of Paul's ministry and the criteria for determining true ministry. The opponents have interpreted Paul's peculiar approach to ministry as "unspiritual," or secular (*kata sarka*, 10:3). Against these charges Paul claims that his ministry of weakness and suffering conforms to the one who "was crucified in weakness, but lives by the power of God" (13:4). Paul claims that his suffering is nothing less than the "carrying about of the dying of Jesus" (4:10). Thus Paul argues that the opponents are the ones who boast "in a secular way" (*kata sarka*, 11:18) while he has left these standards behind (2 Cor 5:16). As one who is in Christ, he has discovered a new creation (2 Cor 5:17) that transforms his understanding of Christ and of authentic ministry.

Although the letter exhibits the changes of tone and the apparent digressions in the argument, it remains focused on Paul's defense of his ministry and his attempt to regain a relationship of mutual admiration that will unite him with the Corinthians (1:14; 5:12). Like the *exordium* of an ancient speech, the opening words are designed to introduce the issue of Paul's suffering and to make the audience favorably disposed (1:1–7) to him. Paul develops his case carefully, proceeding from the thanksgiving

6. Marshall, *Enmity at Corinth*, 74–75.

(1:3–7) to a brief history of the case (*narratio*, 1:8–11) before stating the thesis that will guide the entire letter (*propositio*, 1:12–14). Paul writes to defend his integrity. He introduces his defense in 1:15 and continues it throughout chapters 1–7. After recalling Titus's report of reconciliation in 7:5–16, he proceeds with the request for the Corinthian participation in the collection (chs. 8–9), which he had mentioned earlier (1 Cor 16:1–2). In the harsh and threatening unit in 10–13, he repeats the themes of 1–9 in an emotionally intensified way. One may, therefore, regard chapters 10–13 as the emotional intensification of the defense of Paul's ministry that he had developed in chapters 1–9.

On Preaching 2 Corinthians

In recognizing 2 Corinthians as a personal defense of Paul's ministry, the preacher's first response may be disappointment that powerful texts, when placed in their original context, are removed from the preacher's repertoire. The autobiographical nature of 2 Corinthians presents special problems for the preacher who wonders how to preach another person's autobiography. The specific issues of 2 Corinthians—Paul's weakness and suffering, his refusal to accept payment for his work, the collection for the believers in Jerusalem—may appear sufficiently remote from our concerns to raise questions about the relevance of 2 Corinthians for the contemporary church. However, despite these challenges, 2 Corinthians addresses the church in a powerful way, for the church continues to face issues similar to those in Corinth. Indeed, as Clyde Fant once said, "Corinthians sometimes seem to be everywhere."[7]

The central issue of 2 Corinthians is the challenge confronting the church to determine the nature of its mission and ministry in the context of competing voices. Churches today, as in Paul's time, are caught between competing visions of ministry—between a secular understanding and one that is shaped by the cross; between the desires for market-driven success and the challenge of faithfulness to the cross. Paul's decision to be shaped by the weakness of the cross continues to speak to the contemporary church.

The preacher who at first faces disappointment in discovering that Paul's most memorable phrases in 2 Corinthians are not mere platitudes ready to be served up to the congregation may find, with additional study, that they also speak to the church's own struggle for a greater understanding

7. Fant, *Preaching for Today*, 6.

of its mission and ministry. Paul's defense of his ministry contributes to the contemporary conversation about ministerial identity and church leadership. The congregation that looks to secular models of leadership will find uncomfortable words in 2 Corinthians, where we discover that authentic ministers are the breakable jars who carry around in their bodies the dying of Jesus (cf. 4:10) and find power only in his weakness. The mark of the authentic church is its recognition of leadership that is distinguished by its understanding of the cross of Christ.

Chapter 1

THE CREDIBILITY OF THE MINISTER
2 Corinthians 1:1—2:13

THE OPENING WORDS OF a letter are always a special challenge, but the task is even greater when the speaker faces opposition and suspicion. Paul faces a congregation caught between him and his detractors. Although he founded the church, the Corinthians have asked for his credentials (3:1–3). Recent events have increased the Corinthians' doubts about Paul. The issue of the letter, therefore, is not a major theological issue, as in Galatians. Nor is it the moral conduct of the Corinthians, as in Paul's first letter to this community. The issue is Paul himself. For Paul to avoid the issue in the opening words would not be helpful; to confront his critics would be counterproductive. Paul's challenge is to make a persuasive case in order to ensure that his numerous letters and visits will have good results.

Introducing the Topic: Divine Consolation in the Midst of Suffering (2 Cor 1:1–11)

Paul's introductory words in 2 Corinthians demonstrate the skill with which he faces the issues about his legitimacy (see the introduction). In 1:1–2 he adapts the usual letter form of the salutation to make his case, establishing the proper tone and making contact with the listeners. In the blessing of 1:3–7, he introduces the subject of his own sufferings, the issue for which he is under attack by the Corinthians, in a manner that is carefully stated in language that will not alienate his listeners. The blessing in

1:3–7 is followed in 1:8–11 by a recollection of a specific instance of his suffering, preparing the listener for the discussion that will follow in the remainder of the letter.

The handbooks on oratory recommended that speeches begin by introducing the topic in a way that would make the audience favorably disposed (the *exordium*) and then proceed to a history of the case (the *narratio*) before announcing the case to be argued (*propositio*). Like the ancient orators, Paul knows that the introductory words are important. He speaks to the tense situation with care, introducing the topic of the letter in 1:3–7 and then recalling a past instance of his suffering (1:8–11) before announcing the case to be argued (1:12–14).

Although 2 Corinthians is a highly defensive letter marked by bitter attacks on the listeners, in the salutation in 1:1–2 Paul adapts the common conventions of the letter-speech to establish contact with the listeners and to put them in a favorable frame of mind. Because the introductory salutation is commonplace in Paul's letters, the reader is tempted to ignore opening words. However, one notices here departures from the usual form and anticipations of the discussion in the letter. Paul does not always identify himself as an apostle (cf. Philippians, 1 Thessalonians), but here he does, anticipating the later discussion of true apostleship (11:5, 13; 12:11–12) and the opponents' claims to be apostles. He writes not only to the Corinthians, as in 1 Corinthians (1:1), but "to all in Achaia," indicating his expectation that the letter will circulate in the region around Corinth. As in all of his letters, Paul adapts the familiar greeting (*chairein*) from Hellenistic letters to words from the Jewish liturgy, "grace to you and peace." With this prayer for the readers (cf. Num 6:24, 25), Paul attempts to establish a warm relationship with the listeners in the context of a tense situation.

In 1:3–7, Paul introduces the controversial issue of his weakness and suffering in a way that is calculated to make the listeners favorably disposed. The opponents have criticized him for his weakness, and now Paul introduces the topic in a way that is designed to gain a hearing. Unlike other letters of Paul, this letter opens, not with the thanksgiving (*eucharisteō*), but with a blessing that is also adapted from the Jewish liturgy (cf. Eph 1:3; 1 Pet 1:3). He begins with a general statement about tribulation and divine consolation (vv. 3–4) in his own experience, indicating that God's consolation is at work in his suffering and that the consolation extends from him to others who are afflicted. This reality is based on the fact that both the sufferings of Christ and the divine consolation overflow to Paul

(v. 5). Consequently, his work with the Corinthians is the opportunity for the fellowship of suffering. The blessing concludes with reflections on the community of sufferings (vv. 6–7) that unite Paul with the readers.

The Old Testament, especially the psalms, frequently celebrates the acts of God with the phrase "Blessed be the Lord, who . . ." The relative clause introduced by "who" celebrates what God has done, as in the words of Gen 14:20:

> Blessed be Abram by God most High, maker of heaven and earth;
> and blessed be God Most High,
> who has delivered your enemies into my hand."

In describing the God who "consoles us in all our affliction" (1:3), Paul speaks in the language of the Old Testament in words that recall God's consolation in the midst of Israel's suffering. In exile the despairing Israelites heard the hopeful voice of the prophet, "Comfort, O comfort my people, says your God" (Isa 40:1) and his promise of the one who would "comfort all who mourn" (Isa 61:2). In describing his own experience, Paul identifies with the righteous sufferer of the psalms who finds consolation in the midst of affliction (cf. Ps 116:1–11; 118:5; 119:50). By echoing the liturgical form celebrating what God has done in the midst of the afflictions of the righteous, Paul introduces two related themes of the letter—consolation and affliction—in a way that is designed to reorient the Corinthians' perspective on his suffering without confronting the charges against him. "Consolation" (*paraklēsis*) and the verb "console" appear a total of ten times in vv. 3–7. "Affliction" (*thlipsis*) and the verb "afflict" appear four times, while the related words "suffer" and "suffering" also appear four times. The movement from "us" in 1:3 to "you" (plural) in 1:6–7 indicates that Paul is referring to his own sufferings at the opening of the letter, interpreting his own experience with that of the psalmist. Paul's suffering is not a sign of weakness, as his opponents suggest, but the occasion for God's consolation. At the same time Paul anticipates the argument of the book: human weakness is the occasion for the power of God (cf. 4:7–15; 12:10).

According to v. 4, Paul is not alone in his suffering. With the comfort he receives from God, he is able to comfort those who share his afflictions. The Christian faith offers not an immunity from suffering, but a community of suffering and of divine comfort. Indeed, the epistle offers numerous examples of the forms this affliction may take. Paul experienced sleepless nights (2 Cor 6:5; 11:27), hunger (6:5), and anxiety for the churches (11:28).

The consolation Paul describes is not to be regarded in modern thera-peutic terms, but as the empowerment of God, which occurs in the context of the believer's desperation. Paul's general statement in 1:3–4 anticipates a concrete instance of this consolation when his despair was removed with the good news about the Corinthian church delivered by Titus. When Paul says "The God who consoles the downcast consoled us with the arrival of Titus" (7:5), he recalls the immense grief that his work with the Corinthians had given him. The painful visit and tearful letter (2:1–4) had left Paul "af-flicted in every way" (7:5) until he heard words from Titus that turned his anguish (2:12–13) into joy. In Titus's visit, Paul discovered that the consola-tion Titus had received now had become the source of Paul's consolation (7:7). As a result of Titus's visit, Paul says, "In this we find comfort" (7:13).

Paul is able to share the divine consolation with others, according to v. 5, because the affliction is nothing less than the "sufferings of Christ," which overflow to the apostle along with the divine comfort. Here Paul again challenges his opponents' interpretation of suffering and anticipates the argument to follow. Paul consistently indicates that his own sufferings are nothing less than the sufferings of Christ. According to 4:10, he car-ries around the dying of Jesus. Near the end of the letter, he recalls that Christ "was crucified in weakness, but lives by the power of God" (13:4) and concludes, "We are weak in him." In his other letters, he consistently describes his participation in the death of Jesus (cf. Gal 2:20; 6:17; Phil 3:10; Col 1:24). With his statement that both the sufferings of Christ and the divine consolation "are abundant," Paul introduces the theme of God's "economy" of abundance. God's grace overflows in a variety of ways.[1] The new covenant "abounds in glory" (3:9). In the context of human weakness, God's grace increases thanksgiving to the glory of God. Even a financial contribution given out of deep poverty ultimately "overflows with many thanksgivings to God" (9:12). Indeed, Paul's own weakness has been the occasion for the power of God to be active in his work (12:10). The suffer-ing, which Paul's opponents see as a sign of weakness, is nothing less than the sharing of Christ's sufferings and the opportunity for the reception of God's power.

In his explanation of his sufferings in 1:6–7, Paul appeals to the emo-tions of the listeners, as the repeated phrase "for your consolation" (1:6) and "for you" (1:7) indicate. Paul is a preacher speaking to the corpo-rate identity of the listeners ("you" is plural). As he indicates repeatedly

---

1. Young and Ford, *Meaning and Truth in 2 Corinthians*, 172–73.

throughout the letter, all of the afflictions for which Paul is criticized are for the sake of his troublesome listeners. He is the anxious parent exhausting himself for his children (cf. 12:13–15) as he shares the sufferings of Christ. Indeed, he appeals to their bonds of affection and solidarity with him when he indicates the church is the community of suffering; they share in the sufferings of Christ and in the divine comfort with him (v. 7). Paul frequently informs his churches that they also share in the death of Christ. According to Romans (6:1–4), all believers are "buried with him" (6:2). Later in 2 Corinthians, Paul says, "One died has for all; therefore all have died" (5:14). Paul assumed that believers would suffer for their Christian faith (cf. 1 Thess 2:14–16; 3:4; Phil 1:28). We do not know the extent that the Corinthians have actually shared in Paul's suffering. In light of the issues in the remainder of the book, one wonders if this declaration of a community of suffering in v. 7 is more a wish or tactical move than a reality. Perhaps Paul is only expressing a hope that the church may actually learn to share the suffering of Christ. Despite the pain that his listeners have caused him (2:1–4), their disloyalty to him, and the fact that he is on the defensive for his own suffering, he addresses the topic at hand by describing their partnership with him in the sufferings of Christ. Thus he hopes to turn the listeners away from their secular understanding of his sufferings.

Paul frequently opens the body of his letters with "I want you to know" (Phil 1:12; Rom 1:13) or "I do not want you to be ignorant" and proceeds to describe recent events that are the occasion for the correspondence. Like the ancient Greek orators, who introduced the topic for discussion with a history of the case (*narratio*), he describes recent events that will provide background to the issue of affliction, a major topic of this correspondence (cf. 2:4; 4:8, 17; 6:4; 7:4–5). Paul's recollection in 1:8–11 describes a specific instance of the afflictions mentioned in 1:3–7. In recalling the affliction in Asia, which is otherwise unknown to us, Paul again describes his own experience in the language of the psalmist, who also had been desperate in the face of death (Ps 88:15) before being delivered by God. In Paul's memory of being "utterly, unbearably crushed" (1:8), he anticipates the subsequent claim that he is "afflicted in every way, but not crushed" (4:8). His desperation was the occasion for Paul to recognize his own powerlessness and for God to deliver Paul and to demonstrate the continuing power of "the God who raises the dead" (cf. Rom 4:17). The statement that the Corinthians "join in helping us by your prayers" (1:11) must be read in the context of the tense relationship that one finds in the rest of the letter. Although Paul is on the defensive, he initiates the conversation with this troublesome congregation with an expression of confidence in their good will, preparing the way for later appeals to a reciprocity of affection (cf. 1:12–14).

Reflections for Preaching and Teaching
(2 Cor 1:1–11)

The preacher's first task is to establish a hermeneutical orientation for appropriating the passage, moving from the ancient conversation to our own. This orientation begins with the recognition that the ancient words were the beginning point of Paul's response to the Corinthians' criticism of his weakness and suffering. Since Paul's opening words are intended to reorient the Corinthian attitudes toward suffering and weakness, an appropriate function for the sermon is to reorient contemporary attitudes toward power and weakness in Christian ministry. Popular religion promotes Christianity because of the benefits that it provides. God becomes the provider of physical and spiritual benefits, and the church becomes the vendor of religious commodities. Congregations market their services to consumers who have learned the art of comparison shopping. The American experience has taught us the importance of success in our marketing of religious faith. With the optimism that is characteristic of our society, we believe that our resources, planning, and ingenuity can guarantee the success of the church. If the function of the sermon is parallel to the function of the text, the preacher will aim at the creation of community consciousness that acknowledges the cross as the defining feature of the church's continuing existence and reorients the church's attitude toward weakness, power, and suffering.

One may find the sermon the occasion for reflection on the extent of the call to suffer in the post-Christian world. In a Christian world, we are not called upon to suffer for our faith, but we may observe that Christian faith is offensive in many parts of the world. Persecution of Christians is a continuing and largely unreported reality in many parts of the world. Having lost its privileged place in our society, Christianity is subject to hostility in a post-Christian world. Those who experience social ostracism and subtle forms of isolation for their Christian convictions maintain a heritage of "the sufferings of Christ."

The preacher may either choose as a sermon text the entirety of 1:3–11 or limit the sermon to one of the two units within this section: the blessing in 1:3–7 or the narration of recent events in 1:8–11. In either case, the focus for the sermon is the same: the power of God in the context of human weakness.

Two major options are open to the preacher in the development of the sermon. One may wish to follow the movement of the passage from (a) the experience of suffering as a reality (vv. 3–4) for faithful people to (b) the fact that the Christian faith began with "the sufferings of Christ" (v. 5), not in the center of power. The sermon could conclude with (c) reflections on the church as a community living by the cross. This community is brought together not only by shared victories but also by the sharing of pain. Paul's experience in 1:8–11 could be an illustration within the first movement (a) of the consequences of Christian faith and ministry. This illustration could be augmented by more recent examples.

An alternative movement for the sermon would proceed from (a) the reaffirmation of the Christian belief in the power and consolation of God— a popular theme in American Christianity— to (b) the focus on human weakness as the arena where the power of God is experienced. The first part of the sermon (a), with its focus on God's power, may resonate initially with the expectations of listeners who think of religious faith primarily in terms of divine support and power. The sermon will then move toward the text's affirmation that divine power is not the support for people who need only a little extra strength to get through the day but is God's response to our own powerlessness. The cross is not only a nice decoration or an event of the past. It is the ongoing experience of the church. Here, in the path of suffering, we follow a long tradition that extends from the righteous sufferer of the psalmist, to Jesus Christ, to our own experience. The cross symbolizes powerlessness and self-sacrifice. Thus the passage confronts us, as it confronted the Corinthians, with a word that we would prefer not to hear, with a reorientation of our view of religious faith.

Paul's Travel Plans as a Demonstration of His Desire for Mutual Joy (2 Cor 1:12—2:13)

After obliquely introducing the issue that will dominate the epistle in 1:1–11, Paul comes directly to the issue at hand in the autobiographical section in 1:12—2:13. As one whose integrity is under attack, Paul writes to set the record straight. The tone is defensive. As in his other epistles, he announces the thesis of the entire letter in 1:12–14—what the orators called the *propositio*. He employs the past tense to summarize his ministry (1:12) before describing in the present tense the principle that governs his entire ministry (1:13–14). In 1:15—2:13 he returns to the past tense, applying this principle of his ministry to recent events in his relationship to the Corinthians. Since these recent events have added to the suspicions against him, Paul now places these events in a new light.

The Guiding Principles of Paul's Ministry (2 Cor 1:12–14)

In the face of attacks on his conduct, Paul lays out the guiding principles of his ministry, speaking of his "boast"—what he is "proud of" in his ministry. The dominant thread in this self-defense is not only his integrity, of which he boasts in 1:12, but the fact that his actions have been for the sake of his Corinthian listeners. He has acted with sincerity "especially to [them]" (1:12), and he writes so that "[they] will understand" (1:13). His ultimate aim is that the Corinthians will proceed from the partial understanding of their previous communication to a fuller understanding of the bonds that unite them with him in a common destiny (1:14). At the heart of 2 Corinthians, as these opening words indicate, is the apostle's desire not only to vindicate himself against his attackers but also to reclaim a community that has been caught between Paul and his opponents.

Although in other circumstances Paul speaks negatively of boasting (cf. Rom 3:27; 1 Cor 3:21; 2 Cor 10:12–18), in 2 Corinthians his opponents have forced him into competitive boasting. The issue of the entire epistle is Paul's need to respond to those who boast "in outward appearance" (5:12), describing their many achievements and comparing themselves to Paul (cf. 10:12; 11:12, 16, 18). Forms of the word *boast* (*kauchaomai, kauchēma*) appear nineteen times in chapters 10–13. Closely related to Paul's personal boast is the focus on self-commendation and comparison, a consistent theme throughout the letter (5:12; 6:4; 10:12, 18; 12:11). Paul writes the most autobiographical of his letters because his opponents have forced this exercise in self-justification. The resumé that he offers twice (2 Cor 6:4–10; 11:23–33) elaborates on his personal defense.

In response to his opponents' boasting, Paul will offer his own boast, as the threefold use of the term in 1:12–14 indicates. At issue in the epistle, as the letter's thesis statement indicates in 1:12, is Paul's conduct. He is proud that he has behaved with "frankness and godly sincerity, not by earthly wisdom but by the grace of God." This claim is a response to the opponents' charge that he is insincere, making his plans "according to ordinary human standards" (1:17; cf. 10:24). Paul insists repeatedly throughout the letter that he acts to ensure that no one could doubt his integrity (2:17; cf. 6:3–4; 7:2–4; 8:16–24). He is not, as the opponents suggest, duplicitous. Paul's concern is more than self-justification, however. He writes so that they will come to understand that Paul is their boast just as they are his boast (v. 14). That Paul's churches are his "boast" is a theme in 2 Corinthians and in the other epistles. He expresses his deep affection for this community in 7:4 when he says, "I often boast about you; I have great pride in you; I am filled with consolation." He motivates them to participate in the collection by recalling that he boasts of them (8:24—9:5). Elsewhere in his epistles, he writes that his churches are his "joy and crown" (Phil 4:1; cf. 1 Thess 2:19). Thus Paul is the anxious parent who is motivated by his affection for his children, who can be the source of both his anxiety and of his joy.

Paul writes to ensure that the Corinthians will reciprocate the pride that he takes in them: "that we are your boast." Paul's personal boasts are intended to give his listeners the resource to boast on his behalf (2 Cor 5:12) and to commend him (12:11) to others. The purpose of the letter, as 1:14 indicates, is also the purpose of his ministry. Paul looks toward the "day of the Lord Jesus" in hope that he and the congregation can reciprocate their pride in each other. The goal of his ministry is the formation of communities until the final day. He hopes that they can overcome the obstacles in their relationship caused by the doubts raised by the opponents about his ministry. By focusing on "the day of the Lord Jesus," Paul indicates that his congregations are presently unfinished work and that the ultimate test of his ministry can be measured at the end.

Reflections for Preaching and Teaching (2 Cor 1:12–14)

Paul's philosophy of ministry in 2 Corinthians presents a significant challenge for the minister, for the text is such a personal communication between Paul and his congregation that the preacher may be reticent to preach from it. The autobiography, which is pervasive in 2 Corinthians, also presents a challenge for the preacher for two reasons. In the first place, the autobiography is Paul's, not our own. In the second place, preachers in our own culture are reticent to speak autobiographically. However, issues in our own congregation may provide a hermeneutical orientation that compels us to adapt Paul's autobiography to our own. In the popular mind, preachers are paid to advocate Christianity. We face skepticism about leaders in general and preachers in particular. Professionalism focuses on the skills acquired by ministers and their capacity to make the congregation effective and growing. This passage presents an alternative view of "church growth." A congregation, with its leaders, is progressing toward a destination. The ultimate aim is to boast (i.e., "to be proud of") of the other at the destination. Questions about the church's ministry provide the occasion for reflection on a passage that envisions the goals of the preacher and the church.

The passage presents an invitation for the preacher to move from Paul's reflections about his own ministry to the preacher's own reflections. Just as the Corinthians needed to know something about their preacher, the modern congregation would benefit from knowing its preacher. Moreover, the relationship between preacher and listener as one of a mutuality of boasting could enrich congregational life and focus attention on the essential purpose of the church.

Paul's Sincerity and God's Faithfulness (2 Cor 1:15–22)

Paul commonly opens his letters with autobiographical reflections. In some instances, he speaks autobiographically because he knows, as the oratorical handbooks explain, that the most persuasive case is the argument from the author's own character. Thus he writes to show that he embodies the qualities that he expects his readers to adopt (cf. Gal 1:10–2:21; 1 Thess 2:1–10). In 2 Corinthians Paul speaks autobiographically because recent events have raised questions about his integrity. At the close of 1 Corinthians, Paul had promised to come to Corinth for an extended stay (1 Cor 16:5–7) and then to have the Corinthians supply him for his travels. Events intervened, however, causing Paul to change his travel plans (cf. 2:1–4). This change in plans only added to the Corinthians' doubts about Paul's legitimacy as a Christian leader, causing them to conclude that Paul was a man who could not be trusted. One may wonder why something so trivial as a change of travel plans could be the center of a controversy. Under normal circumstances, altered plans may cause some inconvenience and disappointment, but they should not be a major issue. But where hostility exists already, as it did in Corinth, a change of plans raises questions among Paul's detractors, who already suggest that Paul is not to be trusted. They suggest, in the first place, that he is fickle. He makes his plans "according to ordinary human standards" (*kata sarka*, 1:17), telling his audience what they want to hear. Doubts about the messenger inevitably reflect on the message.

Such charges fit the profile of the stock character in the Greco-Roman world. Ancient writers described the figure of the flatterer who told others what they wanted to hear. Plutarch says, "But the flatterer, since he has no abiding-place of character to dwell in, and since he leads a life not of his own choosing but another's moulding and adapting himself to suit another, is not simple, is not one, but variable and many in one" (*Mor.* 52A–53A). Similarly, Cicero describes this figure when he asks, "What can be as pliant and erratic as the soul of a man who changes not only to suit another's humor and desire but even his expression and nod? 'He says "nay", and "nay" say I; he says "yea" and "yea" say I; in fine, I bid myself agree with him in everything." Cicero is quoting from and commenting on Terence's *Eunuchus*. Here Gnatho says of his own practice: "Whatever they say I praise. If one says no, I say no; if one says yes, I say yes. In fact, I have given orders to myself to agree with them in everything."[2]

Before Paul explains his change of travel plans (1:23—2:4), he places the immediate issue in the larger theological context, associating his choices with the character of God (1:18–22). Even such apparently trivial issues as changes in plans are, in Paul's estimation, theological matters as he associates his ordinary decisions with the nature of God. Paul would not say "yes and no" like the flatterer because such behavior would be inconsistent with the nature of God. To say that "God is faithful" (1:18) is to appeal to one of the church's most fundamental convictions (1 Cor 1:9; 1 Thess 5:24; Heb 10:23; 11:11). God's faithfulness was evident in the fact that God was reliable to keep promises. In the Old Testament God's word is always reliable. According to 1:19–20, the word that Paul had originally preached to the Corinthians was nothing less than God's word. God has said "yes" in Jesus Christ, who is the demonstration of the faithfulness of God (1:19). Paul even declares that all of the promises of God—the unfolding story of God's relationship to Israel—is God's "yes." This Greek-speaking church has now made the Hebrew word "amen" a part of its own vocabulary, responding to God's faithfulness with its own affirmation (1:20). "Amen"—"let it be so"—is the community's word in the assembly, the constant reminder of the faithfulness of God.

Words for the constancy and reliability of God are the common threads throughout Paul's answer in 1:18–22. God is *faithful* (1:18), and

2. Quoted in Marshall, *Enmity at Corinth*, 78–82.

God *establishes* the community. The latter term is found frequently in legal contracts to mean "valid, guaranteed."[3] God's faithfulness may be seen in the three verbs that demonstrate the nature of God's reliability. God has *anointed* the people, *sealed* them, and *given them the pledge* of the Holy Spirit, guaranteeing the security of the community. The *seal* was used to guarantee and authenticate legal documents. The *pledge* was the legally binding first installment in a contract. The language abounds in quasi-legal terminology that expresses the guarantee of God's faithfulness. With these verbs (all in the aorist tense in Greek), Paul refers to a singular moment in the life of the church, apparently the moment of their baptism, when they received God's guarantee.

Paul's surprising response indicates that his ministry is rooted in theology in the strictest sense—in the very nature of God. God's faithfulness as witnessed in the cross shapes Christian ministry. Thus Paul's own decisions are rooted in the story that he tells. Even the most ordinary decisions are deeply theological in nature.

Reflections for Preaching and Teaching (2 Cor 1:15–22)

Although the passage is about Paul's own decision making, it also provides the basis for wider reflection on the nature of ministry and the mission of the church. Paul's defense of his ministry against the "secularists" who judge the church's ministry by human standards is analogous to a contemporary debate over the nature of the church's ministry. The sermon may be the occasion for ministers to reflect on their ministerial choices and temptations to ministry. Ministry involves choices, ordination commitments, promises made to the church. One is tempted to be an opportunist, making commitments only to advance oneself. One makes choices: work in the inner city or in the suburban church? In the same way, the church makes choices and commitments that involve promises made.

Paul's insistence that his faithfulness to his promises in 1:15–22 provides the occasion for reflections on the significance of the commitments that we make. Paul's claim that his faithfulness is rooted in the faithfulness of God is a challenge to the church and contemporary culture. If the ancient people knew the stock character of the flatterer, our culture knows the stock character of the "protean man" who continually reinvents himself.

---

3. Spicq, *Theological Lexicon of the New Testament*, 3:280.

Woody Allen's Zelig was a man who was always transformed into the image of those around him.

Paul's Concern for the Corinthians (2 Cor 1:23—2:13)

Since Paul has declared that he is not an opportunist, changing his plans to fit his own ambitions, he must still explain why he did not make the promised visit, for the fact remains that Paul had not made the trip he had promised. In 1:23—2:11 he explains his change of travel plans, indicating why he wrote a letter (2:3, 9) rather than make the promised visit. If Paul is a man of his word, what could supersede his promised visit? The answer, according to 1:23—2:13, is that he changed his plans in order to "spare" the Corinthians (1:23). That is, the driving force of his ministry, as he explained in the thesis statement in 1:14, is that he lives so that the church may be "his boast" and that he may be "their boast." Paul elaborates on this philosophy in 1:24 when he says that he is "a worker of [their] joy." Paul's churches are his "joy and crown" (cf. Phil 4:1; 1 Thess 2:20), and their progress in the Christian faith fills him with joy (2 Cor 7:4; cf. Phil 2:2). Inasmuch as Paul wanted his joy to be the joy of the Corinthians (2 Cor 2:3), he knew that the promised visit would bring only grief. Paul's travel plans are driven not only by the faithfulness of God; his goal of living in reciprocal boasting with his congregations (1:14) is the basis for his plans.

Despite Paul's desire to rejoice in his congregation, the reality of his relationship has been filled, not with joy, but with pain, as 1:23—2:11 indicates. Forms of the term *lupē* (NRSV "pain") are used in this section eight times. Paul's previous encounters, including the most recent visit, had been an occasion for pain (2:1). He followed the visit with a letter written "out of much distress and anguish of heart and with many tears" (2:4) in order to avoid additional pain (2:3) from those who should have made him rejoice.

Paul now writes in order to move beyond the pain of their previous relationship. Someone in particular has caused pain (2:5) to Paul (cf. 7:11). In causing pain to Paul, the offender has actually damaged the entire community (2:5), which has now punished the offender (2:6). We do not know the nature of the offense, nor do we know "who did the wrong" (7:11). We have no reason to assume that Paul is describing the immorality mentioned in 1 Cor 5:1–11. The reader should not get lost, however, in tracking the nature of the offense, for Paul's desire is to move beyond the past and restore relationships within the church. He minimizes the pain that he has experienced (2:5) and insists that the Corinthians now "forgive and console" the offender (2:7) in order that he not be overcome by excessive sorrow (2:8). Paul asks for the congregation to demonstrate love (2:8), and he promises to forgive whomever they forgive. The ultimate aim, therefore, is to restore the entire community to the reciprocity of boasting that Paul mentioned in 1:14.

What drives Paul is his devotion to his church, which supersedes his commitment to his promises. The commentaries, in their attempt to reconstruct the events behind 2 Corinthians, often miss the driving force of 1:23—2:13. Throughout this unit Paul explains why he wrote a letter rather than visit the Corinthians in person (2:3, 9). One may note the *inclusio* that unites 1:23 and 2:10-11. Paul lives for this community of faith ("to spare you," 1:23; "on your behalf," 2:10). He is a selfless person who lives for the church. His joy and sorrow are totally a matter of the health of his congregation. He wants them to see the love that he has for them (2:4). He is a model of love (2:8) and forgiveness (2:10), hoping that the Corinthians will ultimately follow his model and be restored to the mutuality that he mentions in 1:14.

Paul's description of the anguish of ministry and his devotion to the Corinthian church in 2:12-13 also demonstrate the driving force of his ministry. The fact that his "mind could not rest" is an indication of what he later calls his "anxiety for the churches" (11:28). Paul is not only the evangelist who presses his listeners for the initial commitment but the pastor who remains committed to his congregation. His passion for the Corinthians leads him to press on to Macedonia even when he had multiple opportunities in Troas. Paul's description of himself as a minister defined by his love for the community of faith anticipates his later defense in which the cross has shaped his ministry, teaching him that the minister is not immune from anxiety over the church, for one who is shaped by the cross will accept the humiliation and pain of involvement with others.

Reflections for Preaching and Teaching (2 Cor 1:23—2:13)

The center of gravity for this passage is Paul's concern for the community of faith despite the anguish of ministry. In our hermeneutical orientation we can identify with sources of anguish that complicate the life of the community of faith. As a volunteer community, we have numerous challenges to the peace of the church: issues of power, personal and family problems that affect the church, as well as theological issues. We may identify with the grief that Paul experiences in order to share the appropriate response. For Paul the concern expressed in 1:14 is the driving force in all of his decisions. Because the church is unfinished business, he will accept abuse and challenge the church to move beyond past grievances.

A direction for the sermon is to focus on 1:23—2:13 and to observe a ministry shaped by the story we tell. Because Christ gave himself for us, we devote ourselves to the well-being of the community. The sermon may focus on the countercultural existence that is determined by a concern for others. Paul offers himself as a model of one whose decisions reflected his desire for the good of the Christian community. The sermon is the occasion for reflecting on Christian practice in North America, where basic loyalty to a tradition is diminishing and where the marketing of religion offers benefits without pain. The sermon will move from reflections on contemporary practice to Paul's concern for the church at Corinth as he was willing to forgive personal insults and act in ways that would benefit the church.

Sermons

A Little Praise Music (2 Cor 1:3–11)

When one of my colleagues led a student tour of important sites of the Protestant Reformation in Germany, they came to Wittenberg, the scene of Martin Luther's Ninety-five Theses. Here he suggested that they acknowledge this unforgettable moment by singing Luther's song, "A Mighty Fortress Is Our God." To his surprise, scarcely anyone among the university students knew the song. They liked to sing, but they had an entirely different repertoire. I am sure they could have suggested countless songs that my colleague did not know. This incident, I think, reflects the cultural divide within the church. The students were participating in a revolution that has swept church music in the last generation. For many Christians, praise music has replaced the traditional hymns that have been around for centuries. We now face worship wars that are rooted in this cultural divide.

I do not wish to join this battle at this moment. As much as I like traditional songs, I must acknowledge that praise songs have been around for a long time and have an important place in the life of the church. Israel had a fair number of praise songs in its hymnal, the Psalms. Praise lifts our spirits and expresses our joy in God. Praise music comes naturally when we see the signs of God's presence. This revolution in Christian music has reminded us that praise is the natural response of people who have experienced God's gifts.

Paul also liked praise music. In fact, he opens his second letter to the Corinthians with a little praise music. Although he normally opens his letters with a note of thanksgiving, this time he opens with the words, "Blessed be the God and Father of our Lord Jesus Christ, the Father of mercies and the God of all consolation, who consoles us in all our afflictions" (1:3–4). He speaks in poetry, indicating that he has read enough of the praise songs from the Psalms to write his own. He knew that there is a time to praise God. I must admit, however, that it is a disturbing praise song. It speaks of affliction and suffering—not exactly the themes I expect to hear in praise music.

To be quite honest, there are occasions when we do not feel much like praising God. When I read through 2 Corinthians, I see what Paul meant by "all our afflictions." In the first place, here is the church that he had planted and nurtured, yet all of his work appears to be for nothing. There were the sleepless nights over the fate of this community. On one visit there, some of the members openly rebelled against Paul's authority. To make matters worse, other teachers had come to Corinth to undermine Paul's work. That is why Paul's mind could not rest when he did not get a report from Titus on the situation at Corinth (2:13). And then there were the beatings and the abuse he received in his role as a missionary.

We may not receive the beatings that Paul experienced, but anyone who has been deeply involved in the life of the church knows about sleepless nights and disappointment with the results. Although overt persecution of Christians may not be on our immediate horizon—even if it is in many parts of the world—we discover that Christian commitment involves paying a price. It is in that moment when we do not feel much like praise that Paul leads us in praise music. He does not limit his praise songs to upbeat moments in his Christian life but offers praise "in all our afflictions."

I know it sounds strange to praise God "in all our afflictions." But this is precisely the moment for praise, for here we discover the God who "*consoles us* in all our afflictions." At least that is the way it was for Paul. Just when he was in anguish over conditions at Corinth, he finally met Titus and experienced the presence of God: "But God, who consoles the downcast, consoled us by the arrival of Titus" (7:5). Despite the anguish over the outcome of his work, he recognized God at work. At the moment of greatest despair, God turned his despair to hope.

For centuries, faithful people have found the consolation of God in the midst of their own despair. At the moment of Israel's despair, the prophet said, "Comfort, O comfort my people" (Isa 40:1). God's consolation is not a nice pat on the back but God's presence in our midst to empower us to go on in service despite the disappointments and anguish. In fact, the story that brings us here is the memory of the sufferings of Christ and of the divine power that was at work in that most hopeless hour.

And now we go on praising God—not because we see blue skies and rainbows each day, but because we recognize that God's power is present when we exhaust ourselves for others. God's consolation is present in the midst of our disappointment with the church. God's consolation is present in the very moment when our own resources for ministry are gone. God has called us to share the sufferings of Christ, knowing that God's presence is always present in the midst of our suffering. And the consolation that we receive, we share with others.

It is time for a little praise music. "Blessed be the God and Father of our Lord Jesus Christ, the Father of mercies and God of all consolation, who comforts us in all our afflictions."

Promises to Keep (2 Cor 1:15-23)

I am not exactly sure when I learned my first Hebrew word, but I know that it was early. In fact, I cannot remember a time when I did not know the word "amen." I knew it was the way that we ended a prayer. I was not sure that the prayer counted if we did not say "amen"— sort of like punching the "send" button when we send an e-mail message. Then someone told me that it really meant "so be it." Through the years I have heard the word in many contexts. I have heard it in foreign countries where it was the only word I recognized in the entire service. I have preached in services where I heard it many times, and I wondered what I had done wrong if I did not hear it. It is the kind of word that becomes so familiar that we scarcely remember that it means something. It is our word. In the reading for today, it is a serious word. Paul reminds the Greek-speaking congregation in Corinth of that moment in church when they say the Hebrew word "amen." It is not just the way that we end a prayer. It is more.

I would not have given much thought to this word if Paul had not explained it. He explains the word only because he is under attack. He faces the cynicism all ministers and church leaders face: that he makes his plans as an opportunist, looking out only for himself. He had told the Corinthians that he would visit them and spend the winter, and he had not come.

It sounds as if someone is making a big fuss about something very small. From his failure to keep his commitment to visit, they drew major conclusions about his character. But then our little decisions form a composite of who we are. We all make little decisions each day that serve as indexes to who we are.

It is not easy to keep commitments—at least all of them. We might prefer to keep our options open to new opportunities. We begin a new ministry, and we discover it was not the ideal place that we thought it was. We make a commitment, but then comes the opportunity of a lifetime for something better. We discover we married the wrong person. We bring a child into the world, and the child is a problem-child. In the contemporary climate, personal fulfillment often supersedes our commitments to our spouses and our children. To become involved with a community of faith is to make a commitment. In the same way, the church makes commitments when it initiates new ministries. Because some commitments are simply hard to keep, we discover many reasons not to keep them. To behave in a countercultural way is to keep the commitments we make, discovering in the faithfulness of God our own basis for conduct.

In the middle of a conversation about travel plans, Paul starts explaining what "amen" means and why this Greek-speaking church actually repeats this Hebrew word in its corporate worship. At first, he seems to be changing the subject—from a defense of his change of plans to a theological discussion about this word. That is, it is our response to the faithfulness of God, who always keeps promises. Indeed, God does not say "yes" and "no" at once, and the coming of Jesus Christ is God's ultimate demonstration that God keeps promises. In fact, we live by the power of God's Spirit, the guarantee that God will be faithful to us. When we say "amen," we are acknowledging the faithfulness of God. It is a commitment to that kind of God.

This commitment determines what kind of people we are. We who worship a God who keeps his promises do not take our commitments lightly. Even little commitments mean something. We make friends, and we are implicitly making a promise to be a friend. We become part of an accountability group with friends, and we are saying that we will be faithful to the commitment to the group. We make a commitment to be faithful as a worshiping community, and we do not take such commitments lightly. We pledge ourselves to a congregation of believers. They have good times and bad times, but we know that we have made a promise. They are a part of who we are.

Now I must admit that there must be circumstances when we cannot keep our promises. In fact, Paul did not keep his promise. But there was a higher reason that he did not make the visit he had promised. Conditions were not right. A visit would have been catastrophic for the Corinthians' own spiritual health. Instead of coming, Paul wrote a letter to demonstrate his love for them (2:4). There is another story that forms our character: the one who gave his life for others. If Paul changed his plans, it was not because of selfish opportunism but because of the story of the one who gave himself for others.

We too participate in a story that forms our character. We recall our story, and it shapes the little decisions we make. We confess the God who makes covenants and keeps promises.

Amen.

Chapter 2

WE DO NOT LOSE HEART

2 Corinthians 2:14—5:10

PAUL'S DEFENSE OF HIS ministry in 1:1—2:13 demonstrated his credibility by describing the pain he experienced because of his love for the church. The transition from "I did not find rest for my spirit when I did not find Titus" (2:13) to "thanks be to God, who in Christ leads us in a triumphal procession" (2:14) is so sudden that many readers conclude that a separate letter of defense begins in 2:14. Because Paul resumes the story of his search for Titus in 7:5-16, they conclude that 1:1—2:13 and 7:5-16 is a letter of reconciliation while 2:14—7:4 is a separate letter of defense. Although this view is widely held, this conclusion is not necessary, for 2:13 and 7:5 do not join as seamlessly as many suppose. Moreover, Paul is not totally reconciled to the Corinthians in either section; he alternates between expressions of great affection and the defense against charges that have been made against him. One may also observe that a common theme appears throughout chapters 1–7. Paul defends his sincerity (1:1-12; 2:17) throughout chapters 1–7, indicating that he does not behave "in a secular way" or "by human standards" (NRSV 1:17; 5:16; Greek *kata sarka*). As the thesis statement indicates in 1:12-14, he does not behave with "earthly wisdom" (Greek *sophia sarkinē*) in his ministry. Chapters 1–7 consist of a series of arguments in which Paul hopes to fulfill the philosophy of ministry that he mentions in 1:14—to restore the reciprocity of boasting between him and the church at Corinth.

Paul's Confidence in His Glorious Ministry (2 Cor 2:14—4:6)

Paul's second proof for his legitimacy (2:14—4:6) is a tightly woven unit with an A-B-A pattern in which he demonstrates the glory of his ministry and his confidence in his role as God's minister. The structure of the argument provides insights into Paul's message. He introduces his case (2:14—3:6) and concludes it (4:1–6) with the same themes. The concluding section in 4:1–6 also summarizes the themes from the middle section (3:7–18): the unbelievers' inability to see because of the veil on their eyes (3:14; 4:4). He indicates the glory of the ministry in 2:14 with its imagery of triumph and in 4:5–6 with his description of the shining of the light that calls him to service. He claims in 2:17 that he is different from the "peddlers" and declares in 4:2 that he is not like those who falsify God's word. His claim that his ministry is a matter of life and death (2:15) appears in 4:3–4. In 3:4 he refers to his "confidence," and then at 4:1 he claims that he does not "lose heart." At the center of the argument is Paul's claim that his ministry is more glorious than that of Moses, who placed a veil over his face that prevented the Israelites from seeing the loss of glory (3:12–18). In 4:3–4 he returns to this theme to indicate that the glory exists even if the world does not see it.

The structure of the argument allows us to see the center of gravity for this text. Paul is not engaged in a systematic theology about the relationship between the two covenants. He writes as one who has been placed on the defensive by opponents who claim that his ministry is so ineffective that he should "lose heart" (4:1). Paul responds to the claims with a description of the glory of the Christian message and the claim that his confidence rests in the fact that God has taken one who is not "competent" (3:4) and empowered him for a ministry that has life and death consequences. Indeed, expressions of confidence provide the constant thread throughout this argument. Against those who criticize his ineffectiveness, he speaks of his confidence (3:4), boldness (3:12), freedom (3:17), and courage (5:6, 8, NRSV "confidence") that are based on the glory of his task.

This sudden transition in 2:14 becomes more intelligible if we see what Paul is trying to accomplish. Paul's purpose is not simply to provide a chronicle of his past movements but to defend his credibility in a series of arguments. After the statement of the philosophy of ministry in 1:12–14 (present tense), Paul offers the first argument for his defense in 1:15—2:13

(past tense). In 2:14–17 he introduces the second argument for the credibility of his ministry. Indeed, 2:14–17 is a restatement of Paul's thesis statement (present tense). In the second argument, he describes the nature of his ministry (2:14—7:4) before returning to the past tense in 7:5–16. Therefore, Paul continues to argue for his credibility in 2:14—7:16.

A Victory Processional (2 Cor 2:14–17)

In the sudden transition from anguish to victory in 2:14, Paul describes his ministry in the language of the Roman triumphal processional. The plural, "who leads us in triumph," is actually a reference to Paul's own ministry. In 2 Corinthians, as in his other epistles, Paul often speaks autobiographically with the first-person plural (cf. 1 Thess 2:1–12). In response to the criticisms of his opponents, Paul speaks in the plural throughout this section (2:14—7:4) before returning to the first-person singular in 7:5–16. Paul responds to his opponents by claiming that his apparent failure is nothing less than a triumphal processional. The language recalls Paul's victorious claim in 1 Cor 15:57, "Thanks be to God, who has given us the victory through our Lord Jesus Christ," and his affirmation that "We are more than conquerors through Christ" (Rom 8:37).

In the Roman triumphal processional, victorious generals paraded through the streets, leading the captives to death. Plutarch describes one scene in which the king, his family, and their friends and personal attendants were led through the streets as representatives of the vanquished as a prelude to their execution. Even the children were led as slaves, unaware of the fate that awaited them at the end of the parade (Cf. Plutarch, *Rom.* XXV.4–34). Cleopatra cries at the point of her defeat, "If the gods of Rome have power or mercy left . . . let them not suffer me to be led in living triumph to your disgrace."[1]

Paul elsewhere describes the Christ event as a victory. Indeed, the only other use of Paul's word for triumphal processional (*thriambeuō*) is in Col 2:15, according to which Christ defeated the cosmic rulers and authorities, "triumphing over them." Numerous translations and commentaries have obscured the meaning of "leads us in triumph," suggesting that Paul is the victorious general leading the processional through the streets. Both the grammar and the context suggest, however, that Paul is the captured prisoner in the victory processional. An appropriate translation is "who

---

1. See Hafemann, *Suffering and Ministry in the Spirit*, 25.

triumphs over us." The passage anticipates his claim in 5:14 that "the love of Christ urges us on" (literally, "constrains" or "holds [us] in custody"). Here, as in 1 Cor 9:15–18, Paul declares that this ministry is not his own; he has been captured by Christ.

To the opponents who have seen in Paul's sufferings the signs of defeat, Paul declares that his ministry is a victory processional. His sufferings are, in fact, the signs that he has been captured by God to preach—"to spread the fragrance that comes from knowing him." Thus we can see how he can move from descriptions of his anguish (2:13) to reflection on a victory processional leading to death (2:14). Paul is not his own man; he has been captured by God for a cause of universal consequence.

Paul's references to "fragrance" and "aroma" may be drawn from the victory processional in which the burning of incense signaled victory for some and death for others. His imagery may be loosely based on the triumphal processional, but he draws on a wider use of the imagery in biblical thought. The fragrance of the sacrificial offering is a "pleasing odor" (Exod 29:18, 25, 41). Elsewhere Paul describes himself as the priest offering a sacrifice (Rom 15:16) and as the sacrifice to God (Phil 2:17). His preaching—the sacrificial offering—has life or death consequences for his listeners (2:16; cf. 1 Cor 1:18), dividing them between "those who are being saved" and "those who are perishing." In response to the charges that the opponents have made against his ministry, Paul declares his ministry is a matter of life and death in God's victory processional.

The extraordinary claim of 2:14–16a leads to the rhetorical question "Who is sufficient for these things?" (2:16). The question appears to be a statement of awe and responsibility at the task before Paul. The question probably alludes to the opponents' questions about Paul's competence for ministry. One should observe that Paul is actually echoing Moses, who also was called for an extraordinary task beyond human capabilities. Here Paul begins reflections on the ministry of Moses, which will continue in chapter 3. According to the Septuagint of Exod 4:10, Moses, recognizing the chasm between the task and his own inadequacy, responded to God's call to lead the people with the words "I am not sufficient." The ultimate answer to the question is not given until 3:5, "Our sufficiency is of God."

A ministry of such importance is not for entrepreneurs. In distinguishing between himself and the "many peddlers" (2:17), Paul responds to the charges made against him, introducing a central issue in the Corinthian correspondence. In 1 Corinthians, Paul justifies the fact that he worked with his hands (4:12), refusing to allow the Corinthians to become his financial patrons (cf. 1 Cor 9:3–14). The Corinthians were apparently offended by Paul's refusal of their offer of friendship. This issue continued to aggravate Paul's relationship to the Corinthians, who interpret his refusal of their support as the absence of love (11:7–11). Paul responds, using the language associated with Plato's debates with the sophists.

The "peddler" was a stock figure in philosophical discussions. According to Plato (*Prot.* 313D), "The sophist is like a salesman or merchant in things which nourish the soul. Even so, they sell and huckster." Lucian says of the philosophers, "According to my opinion philosophy and wine are similar in this respect, that philosophers for the most part mix and falsify and use false measures."[2] Paul appears to accuse others of merchandising the gospel while he recognizes that no one who sees the enormity of the Christian message will treat it as a piece of merchandise.

Reflections for Preaching and Teaching

Just as Paul was awed by the task before him, the preacher is likely to be overwhelmed by the prospect of preaching this brief passage. The passage is filled with striking metaphors. The fact that it actually describes Paul's ministry continues to present a challenge to the preacher who wants to communicate it to the contemporary church. As with most of 2 Corinthians, the preacher faces the challenge of preaching the personal experience of Paul. Preachers will want to avoid the suggestion that they stand in Paul's shoes or that they can adopt a defensive posture similar to Paul's. Nevertheless, in order to preach the passage, we can focus on the following issues. In the first place, one may discover the analogies between the situation that evoked the passage and our own situation. The passage is the voice of one who must, in the face of discouragement, demonstrate why one does not "lose heart" in the context of failure. In the second place, the preacher will want to follow the logic of the passage from the announcement of the paradoxical victory to Paul's sense of awe over being an instrument in God's victory processional. The logic indicates that a ministry of such magnitude is not for entrepreneurs. The church's message is not to be marketed with sales techniques. The business of church is not simply to meet the needs of the parishioners. The passage leaves us with a sense of awe that ministry

2. Lucian, *Hermotimus* 59 I.

is participation in the divine drama. Hence the church's ministry is not a matter of gaining market share.

"You Are Our Letter" (2 Cor 3:1–6)

Paul's comparison of his ministry to that of "some" in 2:17 indicates his defensive posture. This comparison of himself to "some" is continued in 3:1 (cf. 11:18), where Paul answers the charges leveled against him. Throughout this section, Paul indicates his confidence (3:4) and boldness, perhaps in response to those who question his effectiveness and power. In 3:1–6 Paul continues the defense, introducing the subject of self-commendation, which is dominant throughout 2 Corinthians (cf. 4:2; 5:12; 6:4; 10:12, 18; 12:11). In 10:12 the term *commend* is synonymous with "compare" and "measure." Here, as in 5:12, Paul denies that he "commends himself" while elsewhere he acknowledges that he does commend himself (6:4). In chapters 10–13 he equates self-commendation with boasting, which the Corinthians have forced upon him (12:11).

Paul's defensive tone indicates that he has been forced by his opponents into professional boasting. The opponents have not only come with their letters of recommendation (3:1); they "commend themselves" and "measure themselves by one another, and compare themselves with one another" (10:12). They boast "according to human standards" (11:18), thus forcing Paul into his own self-defense to a community that demands to know if Christ actually speaks through him (13:3). Behind this issue, which is unique to 2 Corinthians, is the ancient convention of self-praise.[3] Comparison (Greek *synkrisis*) was a means for rhetorical argument in the ancient context. Paul employs this form of argument because the opponents have forced him into self-commendation.

Letters of recommendation were a common convention in the ancient world. Paul's letters often functioned as letters of recommendation (Rom 16:1–2; 1 Cor 16:15–16, 17–18; Phil 2:29–30; 4:2–3). Apparently, Paul's opponents had employed letters to commend themselves and demanded that Paul "commend himself" through letters to the church he had founded. Paul's response is a classic statement of his own understanding of ministry. In 3:1–3 he describes this community as his letter of recommendation—his ultimate credential. The reader should note that the words "You are my letter of recommendation" are addressed to the corporate community ("you"

3. Cf. Forbes, "Comparison, Self-Praise and Irony," 2.

is plural). Just as the community is his "boast" in 1:14, they are also his letter of recommendation, Paul's continuing witness to the world ("known and read by all"). The manuscripts and translations differ on whether the letter is written on "your (the Corinthians') hearts" or "our (Paul's) heart." As a matter of fact, both renderings are appropriate. The extended metaphor in 3:4–6 suggests that Paul is speaking of the Corinthians' hearts. However, Paul also says elsewhere that they are in his heart (7:3; cf. 6:11).

Unlike the letters brought by Paul's opponents, these are letters written, not with ink, but by the spirit of the living God, not on stone tablets, but in fleshy hearts. Paul has moved the imagery from the letters of recommendation brought by the opponents to a comparison between his ministry and that of Moses, which he introduced in 2:16. In describing himself as the minister of the community (3:3 is literally "you are an epistle of Christ ministered by us"), Paul appeals to prophetic texts about the renewal of Israel. According to Ezek 11:19, God will "remove the heart of stone from their flesh and give them a heart of flesh." Ezekiel 36:26 indicates that God will "remove from your body the heart of stone and give you a heart of flesh." This renewal of Israel, according to Jer 31:31, will be accompanied by the "new covenant" written on the hearts of the people of God. Paul focuses on his role as the minister of the new covenant. The opponents, with their letters of recommendation, lack the vital dimension that Paul's ministry possesses: the power of the Spirit.

The preacher should resist the common misuse of the epigrammatic statement "The letter kills, but the Spirit gives life." Paul is not speaking of the contrast between the letter of the law and the spirit of the law. The "letter" is a reference to the stone tablets, to which Paul contrasts the living power of the new covenant that is empowered by the Spirit. He is probably contrasting his own ministry with that of the opponents, whose teaching is not empowered by the Holy Spirit.

Here the preacher must note the rhetorical thrust of the passage, in which Paul defends his ministry by describing the church as the people of the new covenant promised by Jeremiah. Here, as in Gal 3:1–6, Paul appeals to the community's experience of the Spirit as the decisive argument for the legitimacy of his ministry. Paul has played a decisive role in the community's transformation, for he was the "deliverer of the epistle"—the founder of the community. He makes no claim for himself. In his claim that he is not "sufficient," he again echoes the story of Moses, as in 2:16. As the opponents have argued, Paul possesses neither speaking ability nor personal power.

Nevertheless, his sufficiency is from God, who has made him sufficient to be a minister of the new covenant promised by Jeremiah. Against the opponents' claim that they are the true "ministers of Christ" (11:23), Paul claims that God has empowered him for the ministry. This claim is the thread that runs through the letter: Paul finds strength in weakness. Hence he offers an alternative vision of ministry from that offered by the opponents.

Reflections for Preaching and Teaching

Once more the preacher's challenge is to communicate words from Paul's personal defense to communities of faith that are far removed from issues involving self-praise and rival ministries. In looking for the analogies to our own experience, we may again focus on the driving force of Paul's defense: to show why, despite his apparent failures, he has "confidence" (3:4) and "boldness" (3:12), that is, why he does not "lose heart" (4:1). We find a similar experience as we consider the church's mission and ministries. We struggle not only with questions of the nature of the church's ministries but also with apparent failure. The passage confronts us with the alternative visions today about the mission of the church. It also reminds us of our own ineffectiveness and inadequacy for the mission. The passage tells us that God empowers ordinary people for the task of ministry and that the ultimate test of our ministries is the formation of communities of the Spirit.

The sermon may move from reflections on our frustration over apparent failure to our own reassurance that we have left behind permanent letters written on human hearts. When measured by the contemporary standards of success, we may not be able to quantify our successes. Nevertheless, we continue our ministries in the assurance that God has used us to form communities of faith.

The Glory of the Ministry (2 Cor 3:7–18)

At first, this commentary on the story of Moses descending the mountain in Exod 34:29–35 appears to be an intrusion into Paul's argument for his ministry and an unlikely preaching text. Indeed, Hans Windisch argued that 3:7–18 is a commentary that Paul wrote independently of 2 Corinthians.[4] The passage, with phrases such as "ministry of death" (3:7) and

---

4. Windisch, *Der zweite Korintherbrief.*

"ministry of condemnation" (3:9), has often been read as an attack on Judaism and the Torah. A more careful examination will demonstrate, however, that the passage is the central part of the A-B-A pattern of 2:14—4:6 and thus a central part of the argument on the glory of Paul's ministry. In 4:1–6 he refers once more to this ancient story, comparing his own situation to that of Moses.

The story of Moses's shining face (Exod 34:29–35) fascinated Jewish writers for centuries. Among the rabbis, this story demonstrated the glory of the Sinai covenant. The fact that the Old Testament makes no further reference to Moses's appearance further stimulated speculation among Jewish writers, for whom this incident was a demonstration of the glory of the covenant with Moses. The fact that neither the shining face nor the veil is mentioned again evoked rabbinic questions about Moses's veil, raising questions about the permanence of Moses's glorious manifestation. Paul's commentary in 3:7–18 probably reflects his knowledge of this fascination with the story of Moses. Inasmuch as the opponents are Jewish (11:23), it is likely that Paul is responding to their claim to share the glory of Moses and their charge that his ministry lacks the corresponding glory. The opponents probably followed rabbinic traditions that appealed to this passage to demonstrate the glory of the Sinai covenant.

As early as 2:16, Paul began to compare himself with Moses. In 3:2–6 he compared the covenant mediated by Moses with the new covenant, of which he is the minister. In 3:7–11 he continues the comparison, describing two *ministries:* the "ministry of death" / "ministry of condemnation" with the "ministry of the Spirit." Since the legitimacy of Paul's ministry is the dominant theme of 2 Corinthians, we should not interpret Paul's comments in 3:7–11 as a condemnation of the law. Indeed, the striking fact in 3:7–11 is the repetition of the term *glory.* Paul agrees that the old covenant "came in glory." He follows Jewish traditions, according to which the Israelites could not even bare to look at Moses's face (3:7). Paul apparently follows rabbinic speculation about the fate of Moses's glory in assuming that it was transitory, comparing the glory of his own ministry with that of Moses. The central focus of 3:7–11 is not the denial of the glory of the law but the comparison of the Sinai covenant with Paul's own ministry of the new covenant. Indeed, Paul refers to the two covenants as two ministries. He employs the rabbinic argument *from the lesser to the greater* to establish the superiority of his own ministry. The opponents have measured themselves by a temporary glory while Paul identifies himself with the lasting glory of the new covenant. Despite the appearances of Paul's ministry, with its pain and suffering, it is the ministry of the spirit that is more glorious than that of Moses. Although Paul has no shining face as a sign of glory, he recognizes the paradoxical glory of his ministry of weakness. Thus in his comparison of two ministries, Paul is not engaging in systematic reflection about the Torah; he is affirming the glory of his ministry and the reason that he does not "lose heart" (4:1).

In 3:12–18 Paul reflects on his own ministry, continuing the theme of his confidence (3:4), which is synonymous here with his *boldness* (3:12). In a daring move he contrasts his *boldness* to the conduct of Moses, who placed a veil over his face to keep the Israelites from seeing the end of the glory. Again, Paul either adds to the biblical story or follows a well-known tradition in his explanation of the veil. His primary concern is to establish his own boldness in response to the criticisms against him and to draw the parallel between the Israelites' hardness of heart in the ancient story (3:14) and the hardness of hearts that Paul encounters (3:15). Indeed, Paul's comment that "the same veil is still there" (3:14–15) reflects his anguish over the apparent futility of his ministry, the reason one might expect Paul to "lose heart." He knows, nevertheless, that the veil is removed when one "turns to the Lord" (3:16). For those who turn to the Lord, his ministry involves the freedom to come before God without a veil.

Paul comes to the climax of his argument in 3:18 when he contrasts those who remain veiled with those who have "unveiled faces." "We all" refers not only to Paul himself but to all who have "turned to the Lord." This community of faith, as Paul's letter of recommendation (3:2), beholds the glory of the Lord (cf. Exod 16:7, 10), just as Moses did. Unlike Israel, the Christian community beholds the glory "with unveiled faces." Those who turn to the Lord are "being transformed into the image from one degree of glory to another." The Greek word for "transform" (μεταμορφόω) is the same word that is used in the story of the transfiguration recorded in Matthew and Mark (Matt 17:2; Mark 9:2), where Jesus's change into a radiant appearance is a transfiguration (or transformation). Consequently, the Revised Common Lectionary links Exod 34:29–35 with the transfiguration story and 2 Cor 3:12–18 as a basis for reflection on the glory of the Christian revelation. Despite the appearances of Paul's ineffectiveness, the testimony to his ministry is the transformation into the divine image that is already taking place in his churches. As they are transformed into the image of Christ, they learn the message of the cross of Christ. They grow "from glory to glory" even if the results are not always apparent.

Reflections for Preaching and Teaching (2 Cor 3:7–18)

The major challenge of the preacher in dealing with this difficult text is to recognize that Paul is focusing on his own ministry in the context of doubts about the validity of his work. The preacher should avoid explaining the peculiarities of Paul's rabbinic exegesis and focus on the essential thrust of the passage. In the context of the apparent failures of his ministry, Paul refers to the basis for his confidence before God. Despite the appearances, his ministry is even more glorious than that of Moses. The sermon should reflect the text's focus on glory, a term that Paul constantly repeats, although it does not appear in the passage in Exod 34:29–35. By linking this passage with the Sinai theophany (Exod 34:29–35) and the transfiguration of Jesus, the lectionary offers a promising approach to the sermon, allowing the preacher to include images of glory as a contrast to the paradoxical glory of 2 Cor 3:18.

An appropriate focus for the sermon is to move, as Paul does, toward affirming the glory of our present experience of the Christian faith. One might ask at the beginning, "Where is the glory?" and concede that much of contemporary church life does not appear glorious. Preachers and teachers disappoint us. The church appears to be one of many human institutions. Such disappointments undermine our own confidence that God is at work in the context of the church. If only we could see the kind of glory that is described in the two "mountaintop" experiences of the Sinai theophany and the transfiguration! However, despite the appearances, we have seen the glory in the face of Jesus Christ: we see transformation taking place wherever we see a cup of water given in his name, a people who sacrifice themselves for the poor, a people who care for their own bereaved. Whenever we see people abandoning themselves for the sake of others, we see the transformation from one degree of glory to another.

"We Preach . . . Jesus Christ as Lord" (2 Cor 4:1–6)

In 4:1–6 Paul concludes this section on the glory of his ministry, giving a summation of the unit that began in 2:14 and once more returning to the refrain of the reason he does not "lose heart" (cf. 3:4, 12). The central issue of this unit, as the *inclusio* of 4:2, 5–6 indicates, is Paul's apparently ineffective ministry and his explanation of why he does not "lose heart" (4:1). Paul proceeds from (a) what he does not preach (4:2) to (b) an explanation of why the response is meager (4:3–4) and (c) a reaffirmation of the content of his preaching ministry (4:5–6). That is, he will continue to preach that "Jesus Christ is Lord" (4:5) rather than alter the message to suit the listeners because this message is the dazzling light that has transformed his life (4:6).

Paul appears to be both answering charges made against him and bringing charges against opponents who accuse him of practicing cunning (cf. 12:16–18). In his claim that he does not falsify God's word or practice cunning (4:2), he again compares himself to the opponents, who are like Sophists peddling their message (cf. 2:17). His statement "Even if our gospel is veiled" refers to the comparison with Moses in 3:12–18 and to the criticisms that the opponents have made against Paul. Perhaps they have suggested that his message is so obscure that he is ineffective. He was not a dominant figure whose words commanded a response. Like Moses, Paul faces listeners who do not respond favorably because of the veil that blinds them (4:3). Despite the apparent failures, however, Paul argues that the lack of response is not his own responsibility. The gospel is not a matter that the preacher can trim or manipulate in order to take away the veil of blindness from the unbelievers. If listeners do not respond favorably to Paul's message, the responsibility lies not with Paul, but with the "God of this world," who has blinded the eyes of those who do not see the glory (4:3–4). Paul will continue to preach the message that Jesus Christ is Lord (4:5) despite his lack of success because the light of this glory has shone in his heart.

In recalling God's words "let light shine out of darkness" (4:6), Paul refers to the creation story, indicating that the glory of the creation story has occurred once more in the Christ event. He also refers to exilic passages that described God's promises for a restoration of the people. According to Isa 9:2, "On you who dwell in the shadow of death a light shall shine." Isaiah 60:1 indicates that "The glory of the Lord has risen upon you." Because he has seen the glory, he continues to preach "Jesus Christ is Lord." Whether he is successful or not, he knows what message transformed his life.

Reflections for Preaching and Teaching

This passage provides the occasion for reflection on the church's message and the world's response. It is a reminder to us that resistance to the gospel did not begin with the secularization of the modern era. From the beginning, most listeners did not respond favorably to the Christian message, leaving the proclaimers with reasons to "lose heart." The temptation of those who face resistance to the gospel is to ask *what we can do* to change the response. We, like Paul's contemporaries, hear numerous suggestions for determining the outcome. These might include a better marketing approach to the gospel, a worship service that is determined by the potential listeners, or a focus on aspects of the gospel that will be more attractive to our target audience. Paul insists on preaching a gospel that listeners can disbelieve. His answer here is shocking to a mentality that assumes that the results depend on our ingenuity and that we have the right to expect favorable results. Paul confronts discouragement with the knowledge that he is not responsible for the results; if the people are blinded, it is neither his fault nor the fault of the gospel. He will continue to preach that "Jesus is Lord" because this message has transformed his life. He will focus on this message, making himself its slave (4:5), trusting that it is God who is ultimately responsible for the results.

A Ministry Empowered by God (2 Cor 4:7—5:10)

After describing the glory of his ministry and the reason he does not "lose heart" (2:14—4:6), Paul attempts to turn the charges against him to his own advantage in 4:7—5:10, conceding the fact of his weakness and mortality (4:7–11; cf. 10:1, 10–11) and again demonstrating why he does not become discouraged (4:16; cf. 4:1). The constant thread running through the passage continues to be Paul's expression of confidence in his preaching ministry. He describes why, despite his ineffectiveness, he continues to speak (4:13) rather than "lose heart" (cf. 4:16), and he explains why he has confidence in his ministry (5:6, 8), pointing to the divine guarantee (5:5) of the eschatological hope. He defends his suffering by arguing that, as God's vessel for ministry, he is the recipient of God's power (4:7–15). He challenges his listeners to see beyond the weakness of the moment and to recognize that "we walk by faith and not by sight" (5:7), acknowledging that the divine power is not visible to those who see only weakness and failure.

This unit is divided into two primary sections. In 4:7–15 Paul focuses on the present experience of the minister, maintaining that the divine empowerment is at work in the midst of suffering. In 4:16—5:10 he points his listeners beyond the visible circumstances toward the ultimate eschatological outcome of his sufferings: the occasion when the suffering minister and others receive the heavenly dwelling (5:1–10). As in the previous section, he moves the conversation beyond his own ministry to include the experience when "all of us" (cf. 3:18) stand before God in the final judgment (5:10).

The Present Experience of the Minister (2 Cor 4:7–15)

The lectionary divides the passage at 4:5–12, offering a division of the text that differs from that of most translations. Since such divisions are, to a certain extent, subjective judgments, the preacher may choose the lectionary's divisions, incorporating Paul's reflections on his preaching into the description of his afflictions in 4:7–12. One who follows the lectionary may focus on the contrast between the glory of the message (4:5–6) and the fragility of the messenger (4:7–12). I have chosen to include 4:5–6 with the earlier section because it completes the thought introduced at 4:1.

This unit has a threefold structure. In 4:7–12 Paul speaks paradoxically of weakness and power, fear and boldness, death and life in his own present experience. In 4:13–14 Paul presents another motivation for his ministry. Here he speaks not of life in the midst of death but of the presence of the Spirit and the certainty of the resurrection that impel him to speak for God. In 4:15 Paul summarizes the motivations for his ministry, indicating that it is (a) for others and (b) to the glory of God.

In the striking metaphor "We have this treasure in clay jars," Paul makes the transition from the glory of his ministry (2:14—4:6) to his own weakness. The "treasure" is the gospel that has come in glory and transformed his life (4:6). Although people sometimes placed valuables temporarily in clay jars (cf. Jer 32:14), Paul's imagery here suggests the paradoxical nature of his ministry, for clay jars were the inexpensive and disposable bottles of antiquity. Because the clay jar was easily breakable, it became a common metaphor for human fragility (Isa 29:16; 30:14; 45:9; 64:8; Jer 18:6; 22:28; cf. 19:11; Lam 4:2; Job 10:9; Ps 31:12). The trifling value of the pot is contrasted to the extraordinary value of the treasure. Here Paul employs the metaphor to describe his own weakness and suffering, indicating that his ministerial glory is surrounded by much suffering (4:7–12). Indeed, the reference to the "clay jar" of 4:7 anticipates Paul's description of human frailty and suffering that continues throughout 4:7–5:10. Paul describes his body (4:10) and his flesh (4:11) as the locus of his service to

God. The "outer nature" (4:16) that is wasting away and the human body are a transient "earthly tent" (5:1). In response to the opponents' charge that "his bodily presence is weak" (10:10; cf. 11:21, 29; 12:10; 13:3), Paul concedes his weakness, acknowledging that God has placed the treasure in a breakable jar. Like Moses, he knows that he is not competent for the task (2:16; 3:4). Consequently, there is a definite paradox in the placement of a valuable treasure in a cheap, breakable jar. This paradox is consistent with Paul's earlier claim that he is a captive in a triumphal processional.[5]

Contrary to the claims of the opponents, Paul's weakness is not a sign of failure but an occasion for "the extraordinary power of God." Just as Paul acknowledged that he is not competent for the task but that his competence came from God (3:4), here he affirms that he has no power of his own but is only the instrument of the divine power. Just as he affirmed in the opening words of the letter that the divine consolation comes in the midst of affliction (1:3–7), Paul says here that his own human weakness is the occasion for the manifestation of the power of God, a theme that he consistently affirms throughout the letter (cf. 13:3–4). In his discussion of the ultimate example of himself as an earthen vessel, Paul describes his "thorn in the flesh" (12:7–10) and his earnest prayers for its removal. He concludes, "I will boast all the more gladly of my weakness in order that the power of Christ may rest in me" (12:9). Then he concludes, "For whenever I am weak, then I am strong" (12:10).

Paul elaborates on the theme of the divine power in human weakness in vv. 8–12, describing a continuing phenomenon in his ministry. The balanced parallelism in vv. 8–9 is an example of an elevated rhetorical style in Paul's argument. In the contrasting pairs Paul shows the evidence of the divine power in human weakness. In the phrase "afflicted, but not crushed" (4:8), he refers to the afflictions mentioned in 1:3–7. In describing himself as "perplexed, but not driven to despair" (4:8), he recalls such instances as the occasion in Asia when he was "so unutterably crushed that [he] despaired of life itself" (1:8). His statement that he is "persecuted, but not abandoned, knocked down but not destroyed" refers to the numerous ways in which he suffered abuse for his faith (12:10; cf. 11:23–29). The distinguishing feature of his ministry is the weakness and suffering that he constantly displays.

In each of these phrases, Paul emphasizes God's power in human weakness. In the repeated words "but not" (4:8–9) Paul points to the power of God, declaring that human weakness has not deprived him of his

5. Fitzgerald, *Cracks in an Earthen Vessel*, 168.

ministry. Despite the numerous deprivations that appear to destroy him, Paul is confident that the power of God will prevail. While observers look at his weakness as a sign of failure, Paul claims that God's power is present in his weakness.

This catalogue of sufferings is the first of four instances in 2 Corinthians in which Paul lists the sufferings that characterize his ministry. In 6:4–10 and 11:23–33 he offers a list of sufferings as his credentials for ministry; in 12:10 he is "content with weaknesses, insults, hardships, persecutions, and calamities for the sake of Christ." Inasmuch as the catalog of sufferings (commonly known as *peristasis catalog*) appears elsewhere in Paul only in 1 Cor 4:9–13, numerous scholars have argued that the circumstances in Corinth necessitated Paul's use of this literary form. Paul's list of sufferings may be modeled on similar lists in ancient philosophical writings in which philosophers engaged in self-praise by listing the hardships that they had overcome. In offering his catalogue of sufferings, Paul is probably responding to opponents who had compared their achievements to his, using this common literary form.

According to 4:10–12, Paul's tribulations are nothing less than a sharing in the death and resurrection of Christ, the ultimate expression of power in weakness. He elaborates on the earlier expression that "the sufferings of Christ are abundant for us" (1:5) with the statement that in his ministry he "is always carrying in the body the death of Jesus" (4:10). His afflictions are not a misfortune, but a participation in the fate of Christ. The word rendered "the death" (*nekrosis*) is the starkest possible way that Paul could refer to the death of Christ and is used nowhere else in the New Testament. *Nekrosis* is used by ancient Greeks to refer to dead and/or dying tissue.[6] It is used both for the process of dying and for the postmortem stage as well.[7] Paul elaborates this statement in 4:11 when he says, "We are always being given up to death for Jesus's sake." As the captive in the victory processional on his way to death, he continues his ministry by the power of God.

The knowledge of God's power in weakness is the basis for Paul's confidence in his ministry, as Paul indicates in 4:13–15. Paul's words, "I believed and so I spoke" (4:13) echo the words of Psalm 116:10, "I kept my faith, even when I said, 'I am greatly afflicted.'" Just as the psalmist speaks in the context of affliction, Paul continues his preaching ministry, knowing that the one who raised the crucified Christ will raise those who share his

6. Fitzgerald, *Cracks in an Earthen Vessel*, 177.

7. Fitzgerald, *Cracks in an Earthen Vessel*, 177.

afflictions (4:14). Once more Paul seeks to reorient the minds of his listeners, as he did in the opening words of the letter (1:3–7), to the fact that the empowerment for ministry comes only through participation in the sufferings of Christ. As he exhausts himself for the sake of his community, he experiences the grace of God. By God's strange economy (note comments on 1:5), God's grace increases thanksgiving to God. The resurrection power at work in the context of his human frailty will ultimately abound to the glory of God. Where others see in Paul's apparent failure only the signs of defeat, he recognizes that God's power comes in human weakness.

Reflections for Preaching and Teaching (2 Cor 4:7–15)

This passage is an especially challenging text within the North American context in which we, with our resources, do not resonate with the image of the "earthen vessels." If medical science can give strength to "earthenware jars," we are convinced that the effectiveness of our ministries rests on the abundant resources at our disposal. Hence we measure the success of our ministries by the standards we have learned in the marketplace.

The focal point of the sermon should be Paul's insistence that ministry occurs in the context of human limitations. In the North American context the passage is a reminder that our extraordinary resources do not ensure the effectiveness of our ministry. We may wish to trust our capacity to manage the ministry of God through our own ingenuity, and we may believe that market analysis can build a church. However, in other contexts, the passage is a call to recognize that we fulfill God's mission when we trust God's power in our weakness. One recalls Graham Greene's *The Power and the Glory*, in which revolutionary Mexico has almost succeeded in obliterating the church. The last remaining representative of Christianity is the "whiskey priest" now being hunted by the authorities. Greene's point is that Christian faith survives, even in the hands of one as inglorious as the whiskey priest.

The Future of the Minister and Others (2 Cor 4:16—5:10)

In the eschatological reflections in 4:16—5:10, scholars have often been puzzled by the apparent inconsistency between Paul's view of the future and the one that he describes in 1 Corinthians 15. Paul is not, however, a systematic theologian, and the interpreter should not take this unit out of the context of Paul's defense of his ministry. His intent is not to provide a systematic account of the Christian hope but to state why he does not "lose heart" (4:16; cf. 4:1). Paul's claim that "even though our outer nature is wasting away, our inner nature is being renewed day by day" (4:16) is the heading for the unit that follows. Having described present experience in 4:7–15, he now looks to the future in 4:16—5:10. In 4:16–18 Paul makes a general statement contrasting the visible from the invisible worlds, indicating that the contrast offers encouragement. In 5:1–10 he develops this contrast, indicating that this knowledge of the eternal home offers courage for the present. The "for" in verses 4:17 and 5:1 indicates that this unit is an elaboration of Paul's statement of faith in 4:16. In describing the "outer nature" that is "wasting away, " the "slight momentary affliction" (4:17), and the "earthly tent" that is subject to destruction (5:1), he continues the focus on the weakness that appears to be an impediment to his ministry. Despite his weakness his knowledge that he now participates in a ministry that results in the triumph of God strengthens his resolve and gives him courage for the task.

With the change of imagery in 4:16, Paul continues to declare why he does not "lose heart" (4:16). In the statement that the "outer nature is wasting away" (4:16), Paul is not discussing human mortality in general, but the conditions of his own ministry. To all appearances, Paul's "outer nature is wasting away"; he is as fragile as a clay jar (4:7). The term "wasting away" (*diaphtheiro*) was used of starving bodies. The Corinthians, with their admiration of health and power, would have listened to opponents who said that "his bodily presence is weak" (10:11). Although Paul speaks elsewhere (Rom 7:22; cf. Eph 3:16) of the "inner nature," only here does he speak of his mortality as his "outer nature." This "outer nature" is "wasting away" as it carries the dying of Jesus (cf. 4:10).

A ministry that involves only "wasting away" would be the occasion for despair. Paul, however, sees beyond the perspective of his culture and of his opponents. In his statement that "the inner nature is renewed day by day" (4:16), he reiterates his emphasis on the divine power that is at work in the midst of weakness (4:8). The passive "we are being renewed," like the earlier phrase "we are being transformed" (3:18), suggests that the active agent is God, whose power is at work in his ministry. The "inner person" is that dimension of human existence that cannot be scarred or broken by the tribulations that he experiences.

Paul responds to the criticisms of his weakness with a perspective that is intended to reorient his readers' evaluation of his suffering. From Paul's perspective of faith, the affliction that appears to be a sign of weakness is only "slight momentary" as it is "preparing us for an eternal weight of glory" (4:17). With the contrast between the "slight momentary affliction" and the "eternal weight of glory beyond all measure," Paul again challenges his readers to recognize God's extraordinary economy of abundance that overcomes human limitations. Paul speaks in superlatives (Greek *hyperbole*, 1:8; 4:7, 17; 12:7) throughout the letter to describe the Christian experience of God's power. According to 1:5 the comfort from Jesus Christ "abounds" (*perisseuei*) in the context of the minister's sufferings—even when he is "unutterably, unbearably crushed" (1:8). Just as Paul's ministry has a "greater (literally *extraordinary* or *surpassing*) glory" than that of Moses (3:7–11), the insignificant tribulation produces an ultimate glory that is "beyond all measure." The NRSV's "prepares us for" (4:17) is best rendered "produces" (cf. Rom 5:3), for Paul is describing the activity of God in the midst of his own deprivation. Compared to the ultimate eschatological glory, the momentary tribulation for which he is on the defensive is nothing less than trivial.

Only one who sees the unseen can have the perspective of Paul. Borrowing the language of Plato, Paul describes his new perspective that allows him to see beyond the limitations and apparent weakness of his own ministry. Verse 18 contrasts what is seen with the unseen, the temporal with the eternal, anticipating the words of 5:7, according to which we "walk by faith, not by sight." One may compare Rom 8:24, "hope that is seen is not hope." Again this is a response to the opponents, who were interested in present power and achievement—those aspects of ministry that can be seen and measured.

Paul's contrast between the momentary affliction and the eternal weight of glory extends to 5:1–10, where he elaborates on the hope that is the basis for his confidence. The language is full of the anguish in Paul's ministry. Instead of describing his body as a "clay jar," he now describes his human existence as that of an earthly tent (5:1) that will be destroyed. In the meantime, Paul describes his ministry as one of groaning in (5:2, 4), and longing for, the new dwelling (5:2), or homeland (5:9). He faces the struggles of the present moment with the certainty (5:1) of ultimate hope. The "eternal weight of glory" of 4:18 is the heavenly dwelling (5:1) and the presence of the Lord (5:8). Paul's affirmation that "all of us must stand before the judgment seat of Christ" moves the discussion from his own experience to that of all humanity. The fact of ultimate judgment provides the perspective for measuring the community's perspectives in the present.

Paul faces the anguish of the present moment with the certainty of the future. The language of 5:1–10 continues Paul's affirmation of his resolute determination in the midst of affliction. The parallel expressions "we know" in 5:1, 6 indicate Paul's certainty of his convictions. In his statement that "we walk by faith, not by sight" (5:7), he again (cf. 4:18) describes the new Christian epistemology, according to which he, unlike the opponents, is able to recognize the validity of matters that cannot be seen and empirically demonstrated. His twofold expression of confidence (5:6, 8) continues his explanation of why he does not "lose heart" (cf. 4:1, 16). In the present experience, he reaffirms that this future glory has already become a reality in the gift of the Holy Spirit, which is a "guarantee" of the ultimate glory (cf. 1:22). His Christian experience has provided a new way of seeing: the capacity to see beyond the struggles of his ministry to know the ultimate outcome.

Reflections for Preaching and Teaching (2 Cor 4:16—5:10)

The preacher's major challenge with this difficult text is to maintain a focus on the function of this passage within 2 Corinthians. If we give attention to the function, we will avoid attempts to explain the numerous obscure passages in 2 Corinthians. Phrases such as "we will not be found naked" (5:3) and "we have a building" (5:1, future or present?) are best left for another forum. The text actually focuses on an issue that is relevant to all preachers who have experienced the limitations in their resources, and it answers the question, what keeps us going in our ministries? The passage reminds us of the importance of our moving beyond the impatience that we have with ministry and our need to have short-term results.

The sermon could begin with an analysis of our own culture, according to which our lives are determined by the demand for immediate success. The emphasis on the present often results in the demand for immediate satisfaction of our desires. The abundance of goods in Western societies has resulted in our capacity to provide for our desires. In education we are expected to show measurable results. It is no surprise, then, that Christian ministry is affected by the same desire to demonstrate measurable success. Few mission committees would be satisfied with Paul's confidence within the context of apparent failure or his rejoinder that "we walk by faith, not by sight."

This passage is a word of encouragement to all who struggle to answer why they continue to minister despite apparent failure. Ministries in small towns or changing neighborhoods often lead to discouragement as people move away without being replaced. Sacrifices do not pay measurable dividends. Paul's absolute certainty is a model for all of us who have difficulty demonstrating the results of our ministries. We have a new perspective that leads us to look to the unseen, to God's ultimate purposes—purposes that can be seen only in the future.

Sermons

I Love a Parade (2 Cor 2:14–17)

I find that it is very important for Christians to support winners. We like to be reminded of victory in Jesus, and we prefer victory songs to lament songs. We like to be in a church that is going somewhere—that has the smell of victory. Perhaps we were drawn to ministry by the prospect of being a winner, of leading people in a quest that has victory at the end of the road. Sometimes victory looks like bigger assemblies, bigger buildings, more programs that look like success. This is where we like to minister because we like winners.

The text this morning is for me the most gripping one in the New Testament. It is about one man's ministry. Paul describes his ministry as participation in a victory processional. "Thanks be to God who leads us in triumph." Ministry in a victory processional is very attractive. In fact, we like the idea of leading the parade. We are involved in something that matters.

Paul is in a victory processional. He evokes the images of the victorious conquering generals who returned from war to lead the captives in the parade. The processional was a matter of ultimate consequence. But for the participants it was a matter of life and death. The victorious general led his captives through the streets on their way to death. Paul says that God is leading him in triumph. It sounds exciting. We like to be on the winning side.

But Paul is not the conquering general going through the streets before adoring crowds. He is one of the captives. Thus it is a paradoxical victory.

It is a victory processional, but this minister does not look very victorious. What he knows is that he has been captured, and he participates in the victory as a captive. Victory in Jesus does not mean leading the parade. It means being captured—even looking like a loser. Paul sees victory where others see only defeat. He appears to be in a string of failures that do not look like a victory.

Ministry is a matter of cosmic importance, but it does not look very much like it. Frederick Buechner recalls the occasion when he decided to become a minister. He had come from a secular family where ministry was not highly esteemed. He told his grandmother that he had decided to become a minister. She replied, "Was this your idea, or were you just badly advised?"

For us it is an awesome experience to be involved in God's victory processional even if we are the captives. That is why Paul says, "Who is sufficient for these things?" We plan to be ministers for a cause that is so important. "Who is sufficient for these things?" A job that important is surely too important for us!

George Plimpton has made a career of participating in his fantasies in a way that most of us could only wish that we could. He is just an ordinary guy, but on one occasion he suited up with an NFL team and actually played a few downs with the team. On another occasion, he joined a major league baseball team for a day and pretended that he belonged.

I have heard of baseball camps where ordinary people pay extraordinary amounts to go to baseball camp with major leaguers. It is a way of living out their fantasies when they are out of their league. To be involved in ministry is, in one sense, to be out of our league. To think that we can actually declare the word of God is presumption. To think that we can make a difference in the lives of people is presumption. To think that we can be involved in matters of life and death is presumption. Who is sufficient for these things? We are out of our league.

I wonder if I should admit that we, in participating in God's victory processional, are out of our league. I believe it is good to know that. It is good to know this because it keeps us from treating our ministries like merchandise. Like one of the professions. We cannot be peddlers of God's word if we realize that we have been called for a task in which we are out of our league.

It is also good because we are reminded that there is an answer to the question "Who is sufficient?" God uses ordinary people to do ordinary things. He has made us sufficient.

It is also good because it lets us know that we are in a victory processional when we do not feel very victorious. We are here because we have been captured.

I sometimes wonder how ministries go wrong when we are actually nothing less than captives in the victory processional. I wonder if things go wrong because we forget that we are not leading the parade but simply captives in it. I wonder if we forget that we are indeed out of our league in our ministries. Nevertheless, God has called and equipped us for service.

Jesus Christ Is Lord (2 Cor 4:1–6)

When someone says "We do not lose heart," as Paul does in 2 Corinthians, I wonder if that person protests too much. I wonder even more when I see the same words repeated a few lines later in the same chapter (4:16). We are most likely to say "I'm not discouraged" when we have every reason to be discouraged. Churchill did not make his unforgettable "We shall never give up" speech to the British people when the tide had turned in the war but when circumstances were so desperate that giving up was the only logical response to the gravity of the situation. Similarly, Paul protests a bit much when he repeats "We do not lose heart." As much as we may think of the Christian movement as a march to triumph in the beginning, Paul's words indicate otherwise. His movement was going nowhere.

His words should get our attention, for we have every reason to wonder about the future of the church. We ask the questions on a global scale. Philip Jenkins's book *The Next Christendom* describes the decline of Christianity in Europe and North America while it is expanding in the southern hemisphere. We know this experience at the local level also. Many of us recall an earlier time when our churches were thriving, and we wonder why the church has lost its attractiveness in our secular culture.

Churches are responding to this situation in many different ways. For some, this situation is only a matter of packaging. We learn from our consumer culture to market the product in a way that appeals to consumer tastes. One writer has spoken of the "McDonaldization" of American religion. Or we learn from the political sphere to reshape or trim our message to meet the demands of our audience. This is a tempting solution. It is especially tempting when we notice that these responses seem to work. Some appear to have done rather well by offering the message that sells to a consumer-oriented culture.

This was the situation that Paul faced. Others were doing rather well, and he had to explain why his results were meager. I am sure that he was looking around at his competitors when he described the road he would not take: "We have renounced the shameful things that one hides; we refuse to practice cunning or to falsify God's word." His message was not something to manipulate for the sake of audience response.

He confronts the problem: How do we deal with the obvious lack of results? Many people simply reject the message. But Paul does not take responsibility for the results: "If our gospel is veiled, it is veiled for those who are perishing." He goes on to speak of the blindness of those who do not believe. As a matter of fact, he recalls that the history of God's people is not only one of triumph but of discouragement for God's spokespersons. I am not sure I understand what Paul means when he says that "the God of this world has blinded" those who do not listen. But I understand this much. The speaker is not responsible for the results. The gospel is not a message so innocuous that everyone will agree with it. Moses gave God's message to the people, and they rejected it on many occasions. Jesus announced the kingdom, but most people did not receive it. To speak the Christian message is to offer something that many people will not believe!

Nevertheless, with Paul, we know what our message is. "We preach not ourselves, but Jesus Christ as Lord." Whatever the response, we know what our message is. In a culture that has many competing "lords," we preach "Jesus Christ is Lord." The earliest creed of the church was evidently "Jesus Christ is Lord." Early Christian preachers addressed people who knew "many lords" with the claim that Jesus, the Crucified and Risen One, was the absolute Lord. Not everyone accepted this claim. But for many this claim was the light that changed their lives. Paul even describes his conversion as the occasion when God's light "shone in our hearts" just as God had created light at the very beginning. Thus he will go on saying "Jesus Christ is Lord" in good times and bad times because the message changed his life. With Paul "we do not lose heart," for the message that brought us here is that "Jesus Christ is Lord."

Chapter 3

AN APPEAL FOR RECONCILIATION

5:11—7:16

A TRANSITION IN PAUL'S argument for the legitimacy of his ministry appears in 5:11, where his defense moves more directly toward a series of appeals to the readers. Having declared in the thesis statement that his pastoral ambition is that he and the readers may take pride in each other at the coming of Christ (1:14), he has laid the foundation for his appeals for reconciliation in 1:12—5:10. Inasmuch as the Corinthians question Paul's ministry, Paul's pastoral ambition remains unfulfilled. In 5:11—7:16 Paul's continued defense of his ministry and expression of affection are the basis for his appeals for the Corinthians' appropriate response (cf. 5:20—6:2; 6:11–13; 6:14—7:1). In 7:5–16 he expresses gratitude that the Corinthians have responded to him with zeal. He reminds his readers that his defense is intended to bring them to boast on his behalf (5:12) and recognize that his ministry is for them (5:13).

Paul's Ministry as Basis for Appeal for Reconciliation: 2 Corinthians 5:11—6:2

In the words "Therefore, knowing the fear of the Lord, we persuade others" (5:11), Paul continues the defense of his preaching ministry, explaining why he does not "lose heart" (4:1, 16) when he appears to be the epitome of weakness (4:7–11). In the larger context, Paul has described the triangular relationship between himself, the readers, and "some" (3:1; cf. "many" in

2:17) who oppose him. Thus in the words "we persuade others," Paul continues the defense of his preaching ministry, distinguishing himself from the "peddlers of God's word" (2:17) who have brought letters of recommendation (3:1–2) and raised doubts about the legitimacy of his ministry. Unlike those who peddle God's word, he writes as one sent "from God" (2:17). He speaks as one who has seen the dazzling light of creation in the story of Christ (4:5–6), and he is moved to speak because he believes (4:12–13). Now he explains that his task of persuading people comes from the "fear of the Lord" (5:11)—the prospect of standing before the judgment seat of Christ (5:10).

In the immediate context, he has responded to the criticism of his weakness by describing the eschatological hope that leads him to suffer at the present moment. What drives his ministry is the conviction that the Christian message involves ultimate realities. His preaching is not based on the results of the moment but on the ultimate results. Hence Paul proceeds to the heart of his defense of preaching in 5:11—6:2.

His explanation that he "persuades others" in 5:11—6:2 is the centerpiece of the defense of his preaching ministry that began with the thesis statement of the letter in 1:12–14, according to which Paul writes the letter to explain his conduct (1:12) and to restore the reciprocity of boasting that once existed between him and this church that he had founded (1:14). Because the Corinthians do not reciprocate Paul's affection for them (6:11–13; 7:2–4), he must explain why he "persuades others," hoping that his explanation will enable the Corinthians to boast on Paul's behalf to those who "boast in outward appearance" (5:14). The renewal of the reciprocity of boasting will result in a new reconciliation between Paul, the church, and God (5:20—6:2).

As a unit, 5:11—6:2 is a daunting passage. Its length, coupled with the dense theological argumentation, makes this passage a special challenge for the preacher. Indeed, the paragraphing in English translations is instructive, demonstrating the various possibilities for dividing the passage. The NRSV divides the passage into two paragraphs, suggesting two thought units (5:11–15; 5:16–21). In *The Revised Common Lectionary* 5:11–13 and 5:14–17 are linked with 5:6–10 for the fourth Sunday after Pentecost. The reading for the fifth Sunday after Pentecost is 6:1–13. The reading for the fourth Sunday of Lent is 5:16–21. The lectionary readings remind us of essential facts. In the first place, one recalls that this unit is closely linked with the preceding unit, as the reading for the fourth Sunday after Pentecost indicates. In the second place, one observes that 5:16–21, with its reflection on the meaning of the cross, is an appropriate reading for the Lenten season. Nevertheless, the extended text of 5:11—6:2 also presents one coherent thought for the preacher. As the following diagram demonstrates, here Paul continues to explain his ministry of preaching.

A   5:11–12—Paul persuades others (including the Corinthians)

  B 5:13 (γάρ) Paul summarizes his selfless ministerial existence

    C 5:14–15 (γάρ) Paul's selfless ministry is based on the Christian story of Christ's sacrifice, which defines all Christian existence.

      D 5:16 (ὥστε) Paul has a new epistemology as a result of Christ's sacrifice.

      D' 5:17 (ὥστε) All who are in Christ participate in a new world.

    C' 5:18–19 (δέ) Paul's ministry is both defined and granted by God's act of reconciliation in the cross of Christ.

  B' 5:20 Paul summarizes his ministry of persuasion.

A'   5:21—6:2 Paul persuades the Corinthians to be reconciled to God.

The structure of the passage allows us to see its center of gravity and the focal point for preaching. At the beginning and end of the unit, Paul offers an explanation of his ministry and appeals to his readers to accept him. In his implicit (5:11–13) and explicit (5:20; 6:1–2) appeals, he engages in a dialogue with his congregation with its echoes of Paul's earlier expression of desire for a reciprocity of confidence (1:12–14; cf. 7:2–4). In the dense theological reflection in 5:14–19, Paul moves from the "we-you" language of his relationship to the readers to a consideration of the church's basic confession, replacing the personal "we-you" with the more generic reference to "all" (5:14), "those who live" (5:15), and "anyone (who) is in Christ" (5:17). With these generic references Paul describes God's saving activity for the entire Christian community. As the structure indicates, Paul attempts to restore his reciprocal relationship (1:14) with the Corinthians and defend his ministry by appealing to the church's basic confession.

Paul's unfulfilled desire for a relationship with the Corinthians is evident in the "we-you" language of 5:11–13. The wider context of the passage indicates that the first-person plural refers to Paul himself (cf. 1:3–14; 2:14—7:16). He faces a triangle involving himself, the Corinthians, and the opponents—"those who boast in outward appearances." He knows that his work is known to God but not to the Corinthians (5:11), whose confidence in Paul has been undermined by this third party. In the statement that "we are not commending ourselves to you again, but giving you an opportunity to boast about us," he refers to the central issue of the letter: his ultimate desire for the time when "we are your boast even as you are our boast" (1:14). At the present moment, Paul boasts of the Corinthians (7:4; 8:24; 9:3), but the Corinthians do not reciprocate his pride in them.

The opponents' boasts are evident in their letters of recommendation (3:1), their self-commendation, and their practice of comparing themselves to Paul (10:12). Paul's statement that "we are not commending ourselves" (cf. 3:1; 10:12) is in apparent contradiction to his claim in 4:2, "We commend ourselves in every way" (cf. 6:4, "we have commended ourselves"). This apparent contradiction is resolved when one notices the placement of the pronoun "ourselves" in Greek. When Paul speaks positively of self-commendation, he places the pronoun after the verb (συνιστάνοντες ἑαυτούς); when he speaks negatively of self-commendation, he places the pronoun before the verb (ἑαυτοὺς συνιστάνοντες). That is, Paul opposes the *self*-commendation and boasting of the opponents but engages in the self-*commendation* that will answer the boasts of the opponents.[1]

Paul's insistence that the church "answer those who boast in outward appearances" indicates that he is not content merely to provide his own theological rationale for his ministry. He expects the church also to engage in theological analysis in order to answer the counterclaims of its challengers. When he contrasts being "outside ourselves" with being "for you" (5:13), he reiterates the "we-you," summarizing his numerous earlier claims that his sacrificial existence has been for the sake of the Corinthians (cf. 1:6 bis, 7; 2:4; 4:15). Perhaps Paul has raised the issue of "ecstasy" (ἐξέστημεν, "out of one's mind") because of the opponents' emphasis on ecstatic experiences. Paul acknowledges the legitimacy of ecstatic experiences, as he indicates in the description of spiritual gifts in 1 Cor 14. Indeed, he speaks in tongues (1 Cor 14:18). Later he recalls a singular ecstatic moment of being called up into the third heaven (12:1–4). Nevertheless, as Paul indicates earlier (1 Cor 14:4–5), ecstatic gifts are beneficial only when they edify others; he would prefer to "speak five words with [his] mind, in order to instruct others than ten thousand words in a tongue" (14:19). The defining feature of Paul's ministry is the "for you" quality. Paul is actually summarizing his ministerial existence as "for you," suggesting his sacrificial life for the Corinthians and his desire for their reciprocity of boasting (cf. 4:12, 15).

1. Fitzgerald, *Cracks in an Earthen Vessel*, 187.

The centerpiece of Paul's defense of his ministry is the profound theological reflection in 5:14-19. As γάρ indicates in 5:14, Paul now initiates the justification for his ministerial conduct as he enters dense theological territory as part of his continuing story, indicating that the theological discussion is intended to explain his selfless attitude to the Corinthians. In the present tense, Paul says, "The love of Christ urges us on." The language of compulsion (συνέχει ἡμᾶς, "urges us on") suggests that Paul is not his own master. The phrase recalls his description of himself as God's captive in the victorious processional (2:14) and the recipient of a prophetic call (cf. 1 Cor 9:15-18; Gal 1:15). The continuing reality of Paul's ministry is the power of the past event that has "taken over" his life (Phil 3:12).

The love of Christ that continues to impel Paul is rooted in an event of the past. Whereas Paul has earlier explained his sacrificial existence in terms of the continuing reality of the cross in his life (1:5; 4:10-15), here his existence for others is based on the death of Jesus as a past event. Paul defends his ministry by appealing to the church's fundamental convictions, in the phrase "one died for all." He offers a variant of the words he first preached to the Corinthians: "Christ died for our sins according to the Scriptures" (cf. 1 Cor 15:3). Now, in the middle of a debate about the nature of his ministry, he returns to the words that the Corinthians will remember—the common ground that they share.

By adapting the confessional statement "one died for all," Paul prepares the way for his interpretation of the foundational story in 5:14c-15. His argument suggests that the "all" of the creed is the believing community, for which Paul serves as a model. Paul offers an initial interpretation in 14c ("therefore all died") before repeating the creed in 15a and offering a second interpretation in 15b ("in order that they no longer live for themselves"). In the phrase "therefore all died" (5:14c) Paul speaks in the past tense to show that others are caught up in God's grand narrative. In contrast to earlier passages in which Paul has described his own experience as involving the sharing of the suffering of Christ (1:3-7; 4:10), here he extends his own experience to that of others to indicate the general principle that "all died." That is, "all"—the entire believing community—share the narrative of Christ. As Paul says in Romans, "We were buried with him" (6:2) and "our old self was crucified with him" (6:6), here he says that with Christ "all have died." Their own personal stories are subordinated to the big story.

In the second interpretation of the cross for the life of the church ("those who live might live no longer for themselves, but for him," 2 Cor

5:15), Paul again describes why his ministry is actually for others. The self-less act of Christ "for all" is not merely an event of the past but the defining quality of Christian existence. This abandonment of egoism is the basis for Paul's ethical exhortation in Rom 14:7–9, when he instructs the members of the Christian community to welcome each other without despising the other, recognizing that our existence is determined by the power of the cross as a continuing reality within the community.

The consequence of the Christ event—and the structural center of the passage—is Paul's claim in 5:16–17 that his unusual ministry is defined by the standard of the cross and the new creation and that all believers exist within the new creation. Words that have resonated throughout Christian history ("If anyone is in Christ, he is a new creation") were first spoken in the middle of a church controversy. The twofold ὥστε in vv. 16–17 ("therefore" in v. 16; "so" in v. 17) indicates that Paul is drawing the consequences of his statement for his own ministry, moving from his own story (v. 16) to the story of the entire Christian community (τις, v. 17). The contrast of "from now on," "once," and "no longer" reflect Paul's own narrative and the determining influence of the Christ event on his life. Paul describes a change in epistemology—from the old existence when he knew Christ "from a human point of view" (κατὰ σάρκα) to the new existence when he knows no one "from a human point of view." Unlike his opponents who boast "according to human standards" (κατὰ σάρκα, 11:18) and accuse Paul of behaving "according to human standards" (κατὰ σάρκα, 10:2), he has a changed existence that conforms to the general statement in 5:17, which describes "anyone in Christ." In the reference to the "new creation," Paul recalls Israel's story, again referring to Israel's postexilic hope.[2] According to Isa 65:17,

> For I am about to create new heavens and a new earth;
> the former things shall not be remembered or come to mind.

No longer will he *know* (NRSV "regard") anyone from a human point of view even if he once *knew* Christ from a human point of view. Despite centuries of translating 5:17 in an individualistic way ("if anyone is in Christ, he is a new creation"), the context indicates that the NRSV has correctly rendered the sentence, "If anyone is in Christ, *there is* a new creation." That is, Paul is describing his new way of knowing. The believer who has been shaped by the Christ event sees the world in an entirely new way. The hope expressed

---

2. See Thompson, "Reading the Letters as Narrative," 100.

in the Old Testament for a "new heaven and new earth" (Isa 65:17; 66:22) has become a reality for those who share the cross of Christ. If Paul's ministry does not measure up to the standards of his opposition, it is because his opponents have not recognized the reality of the "new creation." Thus he challenges the readers to recognize that this ministry that has occasioned criticism from his opponents is rooted in the Christian story.

Paul explains this "new creation" in the grand confessional statement of 5:18–19. As in 5:14, he appeals to the church's fundamental conviction as the basis for his ministry. The claim that God was "reconciling us to himself through Christ" is equivalent of the statement that "one died for all" in 5:14. In the parallel statements of 5:18–19, Paul summarizes the Christian story, emphasizing that God is the initiator of the cosmic drama of reconciliation. Whereas other texts of the period expressed the hope that God would become reconciled to the people (2 Macc. 1:5; 5:20), Paul speaks of God's initiative in reconciling humanity. Christ's death for human sin (5:14–15, 21) has removed the condition of separation between God and sinful people. In the "new creation" and "reconciliation" in Christ, God has fulfilled Israel's hope for a new world in which the nation would be restored to a peaceful relationship with Yahweh.[3]

The parallel statements in 5:18–19 indicate that the God who acted at the cross also called Paul to service as the proclaimer of this good news. God has "given [Paul] the ministry of reconciliation" (5:18) and the "word of reconciliation" (5:19). Paul responds to the criticism of his ministry with the bold claim that this ministry is from God. Indeed, in the appeal to the Corinthians in 5:20 and 6:1–2, Paul acts as God's ambassador, appealing to the Corinthians to be reconciled to God. He implies that alienation from Paul is also alienation from God. Thus the end of this unit corresponds to the beginning. To reciprocate Paul's devotion to the Corinthians is nothing less than to be reconciled to God.

Preaching and Teaching (2 Cor 5:11—6:2)

The challenge of preaching on this passage is twofold. In the first place, we have the task of preaching to the contemporary church a unit that was originally a highly personal defense of Paul's own ministry. Preaching the autobiographical argument of an ancient preacher is no easy task. In the second place, our challenge is to refuse the temptation to cite these memorable

3. Beale, "Old Testament Background of Reconciliation in 2 Corinthians 5–7," 558.

passages apart from their context. All preaching to the Corinthians must be sensitive to the original context but also aware of the way that the ancient issues also become contemporary.

Paul is a model for preaching here. Highly personal issues become the occasion for reflecting on the Christian faith. In the middle of a church conflict, he returns to the church's confession as the basis for the discussion. Paul's preaching is, therefore, theological.

Although all preaching from this text must reflect an awareness of the issues raised here, preachers may choose among various options for preaching the passage. They may follow the logic of the text and preach this immensely dense theological unit. If so, preachers should resist the temptation to explain the argument. Instead, they should wish to do what the text did—attempt to unite and reorient the church around its confession. The sequence of the text may become the structure for the sermon. Part 1 begins with practical concerns in the life of the church—concerns about the church's values, commitments, and identity. The opening part of the sermon may concede that the church faces alternative views of its mission. Almost every institution now focuses on its mission statement as a basis for its activity. In part 2 of the sermon, we show that Paul himself moved from issues surrounding his own ministry to the foundations of the church's life. With Paul we proceed to a remembrance of the church's confession. Here one notes that this confession is not simply a matter to be recited but has a place in every issue that the church faces. These are occasions for returning to the church's fundamental commitments. With our emphasis on self-giving love, we are the people who inhabit this strange new world. This new way of seeing our world shapes our understanding of our mission. In the final move we challenge the congregation to unite in a new understanding that brings us to be reconciled to God and with each other in a common vision.

Paul's Hardships as a Basis for His Appeal
(2 Cor 6:3—7:4)

In the latter part of Paul's defense of his ministry in chapters 1–7, he intersperses the defense of his work with appeals to his readers to reciprocate his care for them. In the preceding section (5:11—6:2), as we noted, Paul concludes with an appeal to the Corinthians to "be reconciled to God" (5:20) and "not to receive the grace of God in vain" (6:1). In 6:3—7:4 he continues the defense of his ministry, again alternating between his explanation of his ministry and his direct appeal to the community to accept his ministry. He explains his ministry in 6:3–10 before speaking directly to the Corinthians in 6:11–13. He addresses the community in 6:14 and 7:1 in the imperative (hortatory subjective in 7:1), supporting his appeal with the argument in the intervening section in 6:15–18. His imperative in 7:1 is followed by a restatement of his care for the Corinthians in 7:1–4. In this alternation of indicative and imperative, we see two units of thought: 6:3–13 and 6:4—7:4. This pattern of argumentation is suitable as the development of the letter's thesis statement in 1:12–14. Paul writes to restore the reciprocity of boasting between himself and the Corinthians. In 6:3—7:4, as Paul defends himself, his boasting for them (7:4) is one-sided. He justifies his ministry in the hope that they will reciprocate his joy in them.

Credentials for Ministry (2 Cor 6:3–13)

Although I have treated 6:1–2 as the conclusion to the preceding unit, the lectionary, like numerous commentaries, treats verses 6:1–13 as a unit. If one follows this reading, vv. 1–2 and 11–13 form an inclusio in which Paul's appeal to the community frames his defense of his ministry in 6:3–10. In the alternative reading that I have chosen, the argument in 6:3–13 is parallel to the preceding unit in 5:11—6:2. Paul introduces the unit by explaining the necessity of his defense (5:11–12; 6:3–4a) and then continues his defense (5:13–19; 6:3–10) before speaking directly to his audience (5:20—6:2; 6:11–13). In either case, we see Paul alternating between his defense of his ministry and his call for the Corinthians' response to him.

The introduction to this section is 6:3, parallel to the introduction of the section in 5:11–12: Paul explains why he is engaged in this defense. In 5:12 he indicates the necessity that the readers may have the occasion (ἀφορμή) to defend him against his critics; here he defends himself so that no one will have the occasion (προσκοπή) to find fault with his ministry. His insistence that he has "wronged no one, . . . corrupted no one, . . . taken advantage of no one" (7:2; cf. 12:17–18) probably reflects the suspicions surrounding his ministry. The fact that Paul refuses financial support while engaged in a collection of funds was apparently one occasion for these suspicions. Thus Paul enters into a long-standing discussion among philosophers about the messenger's relationship to the message. According to Epictetus, the true Cynic is a messenger of the gods (*Diss.* 3.22.69) who takes care not to do anything that would invalidate the testimony he gives (Epictetus, *Diss.* 4.8.32). In 8:20 Paul gives a specific instance of his care to avoid any appearance of impropriety as he handles the collection. He has taken along trusted companions whose presence ensures the integrity of his work. He wants to look good not only in the eyes of God, but also in the eyes of others (8:21).

In 6:4–10 Paul offers his credentials as the evidence that will demonstrate his integrity as a minister. Here, as in 4:2, he "commends himself" whereas in 5:12 he does not commend himself. Paul's credentials include the long list of hardships and virtues in 6:4–10. In vv. 4b–5 he lists the hardships of his ministry while in vv. 6–7 he lists the ethical virtues that distinguish his work. In vv. 8–10 he describes the paradoxes of his ministry, according to which the appearance of his ministry does not correspond to the reality.

The list of hardships is one of the distinguishing features of 2 Corinthians, as I have already noted in my comments on 4:7–16. In this list of hardships, Paul reaffirms the hardship list in 4:7–15 and anticipates those in 11:23–33 and 12:10. As I have suggested earlier (p. 44), the pervasiveness of these lists of hardships reflects Paul's debates with opponents who offered their own list of hardships. Paul lists nine hardships, which he introduces with the phrase "in great endurance," indicating that hardships are not momentary inconveniences but realities to be endured. Already he has extolled the community's endurance "when you patiently endure the same sufferings that we are also suffering" (1:6) just as he frequently indicates that God's people inevitably endure hardship (cf. Rom 5:3; 8:35; 2 Thess 1:3–4) as they await God's ultimate triumph. Paul recalls his hardships in groups of three. The first triad ("afflictions, hardships, calamities") is associated with hardships of a general nature, a persistent theme of the letter. At the beginning of the letter, Paul extols the God who "comforts us in all our afflictions" (1:4). His "afflictions" involve both his mind and body (cf. 1:8; 2:4; 4:17; 7:4). He refers to his "hardships" and "calamities" again in the list in 12:10. The next three hardships refer to specific afflictions in Paul's ministry. Paul's lists in 2 Corinthians indicate how little we know from the narrative of Acts, for he describes multiple cases of "beatings, imprisonments, and riots" (cf. 2 Cor 11:23–26). The last three hardships accompanied Paul's work and his involvement with his churches. "Labors," "sleepless nights," and "hunger" accompanied his insecure existence as he worked to support himself. As one who carried around the dying of Jesus (4:10), he based his credibility on his tribulations.

In the virtues listed in vv. 6–7, Paul indicates that he not only endured hardship but conducted himself from the purest of motives.[4] The parallel between the virtues listed here and the virtues that he expects of his entire community indicates that he is a model of Christian character (cf. Gal 5:22–23). He validates what he wants of them by exhibiting these qualities himself. His "purity" is equivalent to the "sincerity" that he mentions in 1:12; he has no mixed motives. The same root word is used in 7:11 for the innocence of the Corinthians. His "knowledge" (cf. 4:6; 8:7, "as in everything you abound in faith, in knowledge") is the knowledge of God (10:5; 11:6), for which he commends the Corinthians. "Patience" (μακροθυμία, Gal 5:22; Col 3:12) is the virtue of all Christians, as is "kindness" (Gal 5:22). "Holiness of Spirit" and "genuine love" are also the property of all Christians (cf. Rom 12:9). In his "truthful speech" he distinguishes himself from those who "practice cunning or falsify God's word" (cf. 4:2; 11:10; 12:6). That he lives by the "power of God" is a constant theme of the letter. In his "weapons of righteousness" he is engaged in a war against false ideas (cf. 10:4–6), but he works with total integrity.

In vv. 8–10 he describes the paradoxes of his ministry, according to which his entire life is the expression of strength out of weakness (cf. 4:7–15). To those who measure everything according to the standards of the old world, Paul points to the reality of the new world, which we measure by the standard of the cross. One may compare the same paradoxical existence in 4:8–9. This inversion of the world's values is the consequence of living by the cross of Christ.

These hardships and virtues are the basis for the appeal in 6:11–13, where Paul expresses his affections and asks for the Corinthians to reciprocate. Paul speaks of the openness of his mouth (6:11, lit. "our mouth has opened to you") and his heart ("our heart is wide open to you"), echoing the Septuagint of Ps 118:32 ("You have widened my heart," 119:32 NRSV), but laments that "you are restricted in your affections" (σπλάγχνα, literally the *viscera, inward parts*; cf. BDAG, 938). Nevertheless, he appeals for their response to his affection: "Widen your hearts also." This appeal is consistent with the thesis statement of 2 Corinthians. Paul hopes that he and the Corinthians can ultimately boast in each other (1:14). Having demonstrated

---

4. See Fitzgerald, *Cracks in an Earthen Vessel*, 194.

in the arguments his devotion to the Corinthians, he challenges them to respond to his displays of affection.

Reflections for Preaching and Teaching (2 Cor 6:3–13)

Once more we face the challenge of preaching Paul's own autobiography. Our challenge is, first, the fact that this is the autobiography of a singular individual. Second, it is a claim that we can scarcely make for ourselves. Perhaps, nevertheless, we can use this as a basis for reflection. I suggest that we consider as the hermeneutical starting point the fact that Paul is responding to suspicions about his own ministry. The suspicions raised about Paul are also the suspicions against the contemporary church and its leaders. News reports abound with stories of corruption among church leaders. The traditional criticism of the church was that it was the instrument of the privileged. In Dostoevsky's "Grand Inquisitor," Jesus returns to medieval Spain, and the highest representative of the church tells him to go away and never return. Dostoevsky was reflecting the common criticism that the church had abandoned its founder.

The sermon can follow the movement of the text. We cannot claim that Paul's credentials are our own, but we can treat Paul's list as the measure of our fidelity to our founder. Our success does not depend on our place in the public square or in our political power but in our fidelity to the crucified one. We can show how numerous exemplary people, beginning with Paul, have been authentic servants of Christ, demonstrating by their selflessness the authentic ministry that Paul describes. While we cannot deny our failures, as the numerous news stories indicate, we can point to those who have served quietly. We can use the catalogue of sufferings as a description of the church's aim—to foster those qualities of character. The catalogue describes where we want to be.

The text's division into three sections can also provide the units of the sermon. In the first move we can point to hardships that numerous people have accepted in order to follow Christ. We can use not only the well-known examples of Mother Teresa and others but also examples that have not been newsworthy to illustrate our point. In the second move we describe the qualities of character that actually "commend" our ministry (cf. 6:6–7). In the third move (cf. 6:9–10) we indicate the paradoxical nature of the existence of the community that inverts the value of its society, finding wealth where others see only poverty. In the final move (cf. 6:11–13) we invite the church to appreciate its legacy of faithful servants and to adopt the lifestyle that others have exhibited.

"Come Out from among Them" (2 Cor 6:14—7:4)

Although scholars commonly argue that this unit is misplaced, I suggest an alternative reading that allows us to make sense of this unit. If we recall that Paul has worked within a pattern of defense of his ministry followed by the imperative (cf. 5:20; 6:1–2, 11–13), we will notice that a similar pattern continues here. The imperatives in 6:14 and 7:1 (hortatory subjunctive in Greek) are parallel, providing a frame for a section that calls for the community's separation from evil. Paul adds an additional imperative and personal defense in 7:2–4. Thus I suggest that Paul here continues his appeal for reciprocity with the Corinthians. In 6:14—7:1 he calls for the community to turn away from entangling alliances while in 7:2–4 he invites the Corinthians to turn toward him.

In the opening imperative, "Do not be mismatched with unbelievers," Paul employs the Old Testament prohibition of joining together draft animals of different species (e.g., an ox and a donkey, Deut 22:10) to speak metaphorically of relations with "unbelievers." Normally the term "unbeliever" in Paul's writings refers to non-Christians (cf. 1 Cor 14:22, 23; 1 Cor 6:6; 7:12). Since the issue in 2 Corinthians involves relationships with Paul's opponents, he is probably using the term for relationships with them. If the members of the community are to open their hearts to Paul (6:13), they must withdraw from contact with the opponents. Paul makes his case with two arguments to support this separation before he summarizes it in 7:1. In the first place, the rhetorical questions in 6:14b–16a indicate the clear demarcation that separates the Christian community from sources of impurity. Rhetorical questions are very common in moral instruction (cf. Heb 3:16–18). Paul employs the synonyms partnership (μετοχή), fellowship (κοινωνία), agreement (συμφώνησις), share (συγκατάθεσις), speaking in clear antitheses, recognizing no middle ground: righteousness-lawlessness (cf. 3:7–11), light-darkness (cf. 4:4–6), Christ-Belial, God-idols. Conversion involves leaving one world and entering another. Paul is here reminding the Corinthians of his instructions in chapters 5–10 of 1 Corinthians: the believer must clearly demarcate between the church and the world. The answer to Paul's rhetorical questions should be obvious. The entire passage is an argument for separation from those who would be sources of pollution and from the world that the converts have left behind. No one who has been rescued from absolute evil wants to live on the boundary between good and evil.

In the second place, he reaffirms the communal identity (6:16b), supporting his case with the scriptural references in 6:16b–18. Having asked the question "What agreement does the temple of God have with idols?" (cf. 1 Cor 6:12–20), he now says, "We are the temple of God," reaffirming what he has said in 1 Cor 3:16. This affirmation is both a ringing assurance and a summons for appropriate communal behavior as the series of quotations indicates. Words spoken long ago to Israel also address them, as God speaks in promises and imperatives to guide the people. By combining and paraphrasing Old Testament passages, Paul makes a compelling case for the separation that he requires, introducing all of these passages as the voice of God (6:16). Paul's careful arrangement of the quotations makes the movement from one quotation to the next hardly noticeable.[5]

A   Promise: I will live in them and walk among them . . .

   B: Imperative of Separation: Come out from them and be separate

   B': Imperative of Separation: Touch nothing unclean

A'   Promise: I will be your father. . . .

That is, the promises involve demands on God's people, as "therefore" in 6:17 indicates. The opening promise, "I will live in them and walk among them, and I will be their God, and they will be my people," was the divine promise in Lev 26:11–12 that God would dwell in the sanctuary. In Ezek 37:27 the prophet speaks to the exiles in Babylon, making the same promise that God would again inhabit the sanctuary in Israel's midst. In the larger context of Ezek 37, God's new dwelling would be accompanied by the renewal of Israel and a new covenant of peace. Paul assures the community that this dwelling place is now the church.

The imperatives in 6:17 draw the consequences of God's place in their midst. "Come out from among them and be separate . . . and touch nothing unclean." In language reminiscent of the exodus from Egypt, Isaiah 52:11–12 pictures the return of Israel from the defiled city of Babylon.[6] The God who makes a new covenant with the people once more requires that they respond to God's presence by separating themselves from all impurity.

5. See Webb, *Returning Home*, 32.

6. Webb, *Returning Home*, 42.

Just as the prophet challenged ancient Israelites to leave the corrupt city of Babylon, Paul challenges his readers to abandon their alliances with his opponents.

The command is reinforced by the promise in 6:17d–18. The promise, "I will welcome you," echoes Ezek 20:34 and other passages in the Old Testament in which God offers to welcome Israel back among the people of God. The exiles receive the promise that God will gather the scattered people and restore Israel in a new covenant where he will "accept" them again (cf. Zeph 3:20). In the final citation (6:18), Paul reinforces the promise, quoting from 2 Sam 7:14, which was originally a part of Nathan's promise to David for an everlasting dynasty. The words "I will be a father for him" in the Old Testament become for Paul "I will be a father to you" (plural). That is, a passage once spoken about the promised descendant of David now becomes a promise about the community as recipients of the divine promise. Paul also adapts the words "he shall be a son to me" to the whole church, saying, "You will be my sons and daughters" (cf. Isa 43:6).

This chain of Scripture quotations presents a unified picture of the challenge facing the church. The promise of a new covenant when God would be present in the sanctuary has now come. This good news leads to the impassioned cry to "come out of Babylon" with its impurities in order that God may openly welcome them as they return to the homeland. These promises are the basis for the challenge in 7:1, "Let us cleanse ourselves from every defilement of the flesh and Spirit, making holiness perfect in the sight of the Lord," which repeats the demands in v. 17. As the new exodus community, the church lives under God's promises and pursues holiness as sons and daughters of Zion.

The result of the community's return to God is reconciliation with Paul, as he indicates in the words "Make room for us" in 7:2 (cf. 6:13). The issue, as Paul indicated in the thesis statement of the letter, is a reciprocity of care between himself and the Corinthians. In 7:2–4 we hear Paul's voice of unrequited love for the Corinthians. His defense in 7:2 (cf. 12:16) returns to the suspicions that the opponents have raised about Paul's ministry—that he is not to be trusted. In 7:3–4 he reaffirms his affection for this church. Indeed, in his statement "I have great pride (καύχησις) in you," he reaffirms what he had announced in 1:14 about his own boasting (καύχημα) in the Corinthians. The argument of 6:14—7:4 is intended to call the Corinthians to make a clear choice in his favor. The good news of a new covenant with

God summons the community to an exclusive obligation to God and God's servant.

Reflections for Preaching (2 Cor 6:14—7:4)

Our congregations may have an aversion to this passage that we cannot ignore. Its call for separation may offend our desire for inclusion. The passage may seem to conflict with more inclusionary passages that describe God's welcoming of sinners. Many have heard the passage used as a weapon to support distasteful forms of isolationism. Some have argued that this passage is so exclusionary that it runs counter to Jesus's openness to sinners and Paul's own gospel—that it belongs more to the sect of the Qumran community than to Paul. I suggest that our homiletical reflections on problematic texts begin with our own struggle with its content. In preaching this text, I suggest that we begin with reflections on our own resistance to this theology of exclusion, admitting our initial negative response to its message before we invite the congregation to listen once more to see if its voice continues to speak to our situation.

Our next move is to go beyond our initial resistance and to concede that this passage, with its constant echoes of the Old Testament, merely reaffirms a central theme of Scripture: God calls a people and sets them apart to share God's holiness. This separation is the precondition for God's blessing of the whole world. If Israel acknowledges the covenant, the people will separate from the evil that is around it. Indeed, one cannot imagine that Israel could have maintained its cultural identity despite captivity and the loss of its cultural symbols without separating from the evils of its own culture.

Some forms of separation are necessary if we believe that evil exists. Our passage knows no middle ground. Again, we may resist the sharp contrasts between light and darkness, good and evil. We prefer to speak of the "grey" areas of theological and moral discourse. Without this sharp distinction, however, we lose all relevance. The church can scarcely be the "light of the world" without a contrast to its own cultural icons. We might consider the "idols" of our own culture from which we need to withdraw: the culture of success that places the individual's achievement ahead of the larger group, the materialism that leaves people behind, and the nationalism that ignores God's concern for all the people of the world.

Having affirmed the legitimate place for separation, we observe the text's assurances in our next move. We as a corporate community are the temple of God. We do not "come out from among them" as individuals, but as community. Furthermore, we experience the presence of God as we join Abraham, the captives in Babylon, and countless others who have taken the risk of going out from the icons of their own culture.

"Coming out from among them," as 7:1 indicates, is not one event, but a journey toward holiness. It is full of risks, but the end of the journey is to become like the one who calls us. To be like God is to separate from the idols that surround us.

A Time for Rejoicing (2 Cor 7:5–16)

Scholars have long noted that Paul completes the narrative in 7:5–16 that was abruptly interrupted in 2:13. He had gone to Macedonia, hoping to learn the news about the Corinthians from Titus (2:13), but had found no rest when he failed to meet Titus. In 7:5–16 he shows how his anguish turned to joy when Titus finally arrived. This close linking of 2:13 and 7:5 suggests to many that Paul's defense of his ministry (2:14—7:4) was originally a separate letter that has interrupted his original letter of reconciliation (1:1—2:13 + 7:5–16). In my alternative reading, I suggest that 7:5 also links well with 7:4, where Paul expresses his consolation and joy in affliction. In 7:5–16 he offers an example of both joy and consolation as he recalls his encounter with Titus. As he has insisted throughout the letter (cf. 4:7–15), his despair is always overcome by the presence of God.

The structure of 7:5–16 indicates that Paul is here illustrating what he has said in 7:4. In 7:5–6 he recalls the event when the anguish of ministry, already described in 6:4–10, turned to joy. He was "afflicted in every way" (7:5; cf. 6:4, "in afflictions, hardships") before Titus arrived. Paul offers the thesis statement of this section in 7:5–7 before elaborating in the remainder of the chapter. In 7:6 Paul speaks of his own consolation, which he describes in greater detail in 7:8–13. In 7:7 he speaks of Titus's consolation, which he elaborates in 7:14–16. Paul's refrain at the end of each of these subunits (7:7, 13, 16) indicates the center of gravity for this passage. In 7:7 he says, "So I rejoiced still more." In 7:13 he says, "In this we find comfort." At the end of the chapter, he says, "I rejoice, because I have complete confidence in you." Paul is illustrating the joy and consolation of his ministry.

This passage also illustrates the basic claim that Paul made in his opening prayer of blessing. According to 1:3–4, God is "the God of all consolation, who consoles us in all our affliction, so that we may be able to console those who are in any affliction with the consolation with which we have been consoled by God." According to 7:6, "God, who consoles the downcast, consoled us by the arrival of Titus." Just as God comforted his despairing people in ancient Babylon (Isa 40:1; 49:13), God now comforts Paul in the anguish of ministry. This consolation is not, however, mere words. As in the biblical tradition generally, God's consolation is the empowering divine presence. Paul's insistence that God consoles the downcast is rooted in the confidence expressed by the psalmist, as I indicated on p. xx. His conviction that God was present in the coming of Titus is consistent with his constant experience of God's power in the context of his weakness throughout the letter (cf. 4:7). This consolation is the source of his joy (7:7).

In vv. 8–13, Paul offers the details of how his anguish turned to consolation at the arrival of Titus. The contrast between Paul's present experience and the sequence of events that preceded it reflects this radical change. Past experience is marked by grief. After a previous painful visit he had written them "out of much distress and anguish of heart and with many tears" (2:3). In 7:8–13 he recalls the grief his letter caused, but indicates that he has no regrets, for the grief was only temporary (7:8). Because it was "godly grief" (7:9, 10) rather than "worldly grief," it had the desired results, leading to repentance. Paul's general statement about the two kinds of grief in v. 10 is admittedly obscure, as it is without parallel in his other writings. Indeed, this is the only passage in the Pauline writings where he speaks of the repentance of Christians. Nevertheless, we can see the point of Paul's description of this sequence of events. The purpose of the letter had not been directed to the immediate cause of the rupture in their relationship—neither the one who did the wrong nor the one who was wronged (cf. 2:5–11)—but to ensure that their "zeal (σπουδή)" for Paul might be clear to them and to God (7:12). The result of the letter was the news that Titus had brought (cf. 7:7): the manifestation of their "earnestness" (σπουδή; the same word is rendered "zeal" in 7:12 NRSV), eagerness to clear themselves, indignation, alarm, longing, zeal, and punishment (cf. 7:7). The Corinthians had punished the offender described in 2:5–11, and they had responded to Paul's letter with great affection. Painful moments of the immediate past have been resolved. Thus Paul says, "Now I rejoice" (7:9) and "In this we find comfort" (7:13; the perfect tense παρακεκλήμεθα means literally "we found comfort and still do"). Paul's satisfaction reflects his pastoral ambition, stated in the letter's thesis statement, that he and this community exist in a relationship of reciprocal pride in each other. In the coming of Titus, Paul has seen a glimpse of this reciprocal pride: he finds joy in the progress of his churches and their affection for him.

In vv. 13b–16, Paul elaborates on v. 7, indicating that an additional source of his present joy and comfort is the comfort that Titus has received. Titus plays a special role in Paul's ministry, according to 2 Corinthians and Galatians. He had delivered the tearful letter mentioned in 7:8–13 and brought back the good news that is the occasion for the letter. Paul will send him back again for the collection of funds that is a driving force in Paul's ministry (8:16). Titus obviously identifies with Paul's anguish and joy. Just as Paul's mind is often set at rest by the positive response of his converts (cf. 1 Cor 16:8, Phlm 8, 20), Titus's mind (Greek πνεῦμα = spirit) has been set at rest. Titus is relieved because Paul's boasting about them has come true (v. 14). Here Paul develops the theme that he announced at the beginning of the letter (1:14). The Corinthians, like Paul's other churches, are his "boast" (cf. Rom 15:17; Phil 2:16; 1 Thess 2:19). Paul's pride in them is evident not only in what he has said to Titus but also in his boasting about their participation in the collection (8:24—9:5). He is the proud parent of his churches, and he is boastful when they are obedient and ashamed when they are not. Now he shares Titus's joy.

Titus also shares Paul's affection for this church (7:15). They had received him into their homes just as Paul's churches often exercise hospitality toward him or his partners in ministry (cf. 1 Cor 16:10; Phil 2:19–30; Phlm 22), and he reciprocates with the same affection that Paul has for his churches (cf. Phil 1:7–8). Titus's affection for them is the source of Paul's joy, as Paul indicates in the concluding expression of joy in 7:16. While the opponents have seen only despair and failure in Paul's ministry, he sees joy and confidence.

Reflections for Preaching (2 Cor 7:5–16)

The center of gravity for 7:5–16, as I have indicated, is the motif of consolation and joy in ministry that is the constant refrain in this unit (7:7, 9, 13, 16). Paul will not separate the afflictions of ministry from its joys. In his inclusion of Titus, we may find the hermeneutical opening for the sermon. Like Titus, we are involved in advancing the work of Paul, and we share the anguish of ministry. Our sermon does not need to be limited in scope to professional pastors, however. It speaks with realism of the ministry of the entire church, addressing our own concerns. With Paul and Titus, we wonder about the future of the church. We move from program to program, hoping that each one will bring the renewal of the church. After repeated attempts to resolve the many crises within the church, we wonder if our work is doomed to fail. Our passage offers a response to our own concerns, for it offers a glimpse of God's work in a desperate situation. Through the most ordinary means—the visit of a coworker—God offers consolation and power that leads to the renewal of the joy of ministry.

Our starting point for the sermon depends on our circumstances. If our people have imbibed the triumphalist spirit that expects God's blessing to be evident in constant reassurances, we may wish to begin with Paul's joy and consolation, allowing the congregation to connect with Paul's triumph and happy ending. We can then do a flashback to the earlier narrative to show that the happy ending can be appreciated only when we know the anguish that preceded it. We will offer a realistic portrait of Christian service as a challenge to the unrealistic portrayals that we commonly see in American religion. God's power and consolation come not to those who are already triumphant but to those who experience anguish about the church's future. Therefore, the sermon can move from the announcement of victory and joy to the anguish of ministry before returning to the announcement of joy in our ministry.

If, however, we experience despair over the church, we begin with the anguish of 7:5, identifying Paul's concern about the future of the church with our own concern, and then move toward the reassurance that the passage offers. We are often sustained by the occasions when anguish turns to consolation. We discover the hand of God on occasions when our work has led only to disappointment.

Sermons

A New World (2 Cor 5:11—6:2)

"Do you know what the two most common features of growing churches are?" someone asked in a church meeting not long ago. "They are music and drama." He added, "The people we are trying to reach connect only with contemporary music; the traditional worship service, with its emphasis on preaching, leaves them cold." Perhaps he was right. I am not here to settle the worship wars, and I know that we, like almost every congregation, have different views on the subject. In fact, I have been in enough church meetings to know that we hold to very different views about many things that concern the church. One needs only to attend a budget meeting to recognize that we hold very different views about our mission. Do we exist to bring justice to the poor or to save souls? To get involved in political issues of one party or the other or to attend to more spiritual things? While we can appreciate diversity, there are occasions when we have to begin a conversation about the values that make us a community. Perhaps we can begin a conversation that provides a basis for the conversation about who we are.

Our problem is not a new one. It was the same way when Paul wrote 2 Corinthians. If we overhear the conversation between Paul and the Corinthians, we are likely to hear a conversation that sounds like our own. Many of the Corinthians did not know what to make of Paul's ministry. He did not measure up to the standards of leadership that they had come to expect. The results were meager, and he had little to show for his exhausting work. Paul knew that they could not live forever with differing standards of leadership, and so he pauses to explain himself. "For if we are beside ourselves, it is for God; if we are in our right mind, it is for you." Perhaps he did not have much to show for his labor, but he knew that the "for you" quality determined his ministry. If we overhear a conversation between Paul and this church that he founded, we may gain insights for our own questions.

Why does Paul define ministry as "for you?" He offers a very simple answer, explaining his entire ministry with the simple phrase "One died for all; therefore all died." We know that phrase, of course. It is a variation of a statement of faith that we hear on almost every page of the New Testament. In fact, the first announcement of the Christian faith that the Corinthians received was "Christ died for our sins according to the Scriptures." Now, in the heat of the discussion about the church's mission, Paul says "one died for all." Imagine being in a church that is attempting to decide between construction of a new family life center and opening a soup kitchen, and someone says, "Don't forget. One died for all."

Paul offers this reminder of the church's most fundamental conviction because that story is not only a creed to be recited but also the church's foundation. The cross is not only an item to hang tastefully in the sanctuary but the governing story for the church's existence. That is why he adds to the words "One died for all" his own commentary: "Therefore all died."

Then he adds "so that they no longer live to themselves, but for the one who died and was raised for them." The story has a vital place in our budget decisions or when we engage in worship wars, for it is the one story we all share—our mission statement as a community.

I was amused last year when Dilbert, the cartoon character who inhabits the little cubicle that is familiar to many of us, had to stop what he was doing because the boss suddenly asked him to write a mission statement. Along with my colleagues, I connected with that scene because I seem to be involved in hours of meetings to write a mission statement for my university, my department, and every other area that I am involved in. I would prefer to get on with business without pausing to consider a mission statement. However, I understand the current emphasis on mission statements. Institutions go on aimlessly without recalling what they are really about. They often have unspoken and conflicting assumptions about their mission. The church, like other institutions, can get caught up in thinking its only purpose is to perpetuate itself or to gain market share, forgetting its mission. We may not settle our disputes, but we can return to the foundation that we all share: "One died for all; therefore all died." The story of the selfless Christ becomes the story of a community. Those who recite "suffered under Pontius Pilate" become transformed to think of something other than their own demands. The next time we begin to discuss the direction of the church, I hope I remember to say, "One died for all; therefore all died."

I understand that this way of thinking does not make much sense. Practically every message that we absorb in our society tells us otherwise. But then Paul knows that it does not make much sense. That is why he adds, "If anyone is in Christ, there is a new creation." I know that most translations have rendered Paul's statement, "If anyone is in Christ, he is a new creature." But the NRSV gives the appropriate translation: "If anyone is in Christ, there is a new creation." In Christ we have a totally new way of knowing and seeing. Things that once made no sense now make sense to us. Dying to ourselves seems senseless in a culture of narcissism; it does not fit well with our culture of competition and ambition. A woman spends her life in the slums of Calcutta for the sake of others—it makes sense only to those who have seen a new world. A church decides that there is something more to its mission than competing for market share; it remains in a changing neighborhood when good sense says that the prudent thing to do is to move to the more friendly environment of the suburbs. A family accepts a lower standard of living in order to have time for aged parents. It makes sense only when we recall that our faith began when "one died for all." That story shapes us in many ways.

This is a strange way of looking at things, but it is from God. That is why Paul says, "All this is from God, who reconciles the world to himself. That is, God was in Christ reconciling the world to himself, and has given us the word of reconciliation." God has given us a mission. Perhaps our plans and ministries, if we have heard that story, will not make much sense. We can say only, "Be reconciled to God," even though we do not know our prospects for being heard. Let us remember the story we tell. It will determine the kind of church we want to be.

The Pursuit of Happiness (2 Cor 7:5–16)

"Rejoice in the Lord. Again I say rejoice." Those words from Philippians (4:4) resonate with us. Public opinion and movie stereotypes may suggest that we must choose between the joy of living—the *joie de vivre*—and the Christian faith. However, we do not want to choose. The "pursuit of happiness" is a goal that is enshrined in our Declaration of Independence, and we want to share in it. Although we face the persistent suspicion that our faith takes the joy out of life by speaking of self-denial and a cross, we discover the consistent claim in the New Testament that our faith brings what Paul calls "the joy and peace of believing" (Rom 15:3). In the middle of 2 Corinthians, Paul repeats the refrain "I rejoiced still more" (7:7). "Now I rejoice" (7:9). "I rejoice, because I have complete confidence in you." This is a religion of joy.

From the very beginning, Christians expressed their joy through singing because they have something to sing about. From the children's song "Blue Skies and Rainbows" to Beethoven's "Joyful, Joyful We Adore Thee," we like to "rejoice in the Lord" through music. But I must admit that I wish I could say that "the joy of believing" was the whole story. There are times when most of us do not feel like singing. Truth in advertising compels me to admit that we experience more in life than "blue skies and rainbows." In fact, the Christian faith brings on a considerable amount of anguish that we otherwise could avoid. At least, that is the way it was with Paul.

Paul's expression of joy comes only after a period of sleepless nights and anguish over his children in the faith, who have given him little but pain. He has already made one painful visit during which many church members rebelled against him. He has written a letter "with many tears" (2:4) to correct the situation, sending Titus to deliver Paul's message. Then there was the moment when he had planned to meet with Titus to find out the results of Titus's visit. His mind "could not rest" because he failed to find Titus. In fact, this sequence of events is not the only instance of the anguish that accompanied Paul's service. He experienced "afflictions, hardships, calamities, beatings, imprisonments, riots, labors, sleepless nights, hunger" (6:4–5), and numerous other hardships. His faith brought hostility from outside sources and resistance from his own spiritual children.

At some level, we can all understand the anguish of the Christian faith because the risk of loving another always carries the prospect of sleepless nights. Many of us recall that thrill of seeing our own offspring for the first time. Then we recall the mixture of joy and anxious concern that would never go away. We have anxious moments when we watch our children through the process that includes childhood diseases, adolescent temptations, and the transition to a productive life. I once asked my aged father when we stop worrying about our children. He responded, "Not until they are past fifty years old."

It is the same way with the life of faith, as Paul demonstrates. To care is to invite disappointment and pain. We pour out our energy for a ministry to the poor, and we then wonder if we made any impact at all. Idealistic teachers volunteer to work with at-risk adolescents and then wonder after a while if they have made any positive impact at all. When we sense that we have failed, we do not see "blue skies and rainbows," and we do not feel very much like rejoicing.

But then something happens. Disappointment is not the end of the story. For Paul the anguish and worry over the Corinthians was the prelude to his joy in their progress. After the disappointment of not finding Titus in Troas, Paul finally met Titus in Macedonia and brought good news. Paul's tearful letter had been effective. The Corinthians had repented from their rebellion against Paul, and they had expressed their affection for him. Here is the moment that Paul can say, "I rejoice." It was not the rejoicing of someone who is unaware of disappointment, but of one who has lived through despair and sleepless nights.

At the beginning of 2 Corinthians, Paul had said, "Blessed be the God and Father of our Lord Jesus Christ, the Father of mercies and God of all consolation, who consoles us in all our afflictions." Only when Titus comes to bring good news do we see the concrete example of the God who "comforts us in all our affliction"; now Paul says, "But God, who consoles the downcast, consoled us by the arrival of Titus, and not only by his coming, but also the consolation with which he was consoled about you." Now Paul can say, "I rejoice," because he is a proud parent who has lived through the adolescence of his children, and he sees that his work among the Corinthians was worthwhile.

Many of us know the delight of a relationship with our children after the turbulence of their adolescent years. When we have the enjoyment of this relationship, we know that all of the risks of loving and the anxieties over their outcome were worth it. I am sure the very fact that we maintain our commitment to the life of the church reflects the fact that "Titus" has come to us with the good news that it was worth it. I have had those occasions when "Titus" came to bring God's consolation in the context of disappointment. Many in our culture try the "pursuit of happiness" without risk or commitment. We have found in the God who "consoles us in all our afflictions" the real source of joy.

Chapter 4

THE GRACE THAT CONTINUES
2 Corinthians 8–9

A COMMON FEATURE OF Paul's letters is the movement of the argument from
the theological foundation to the response that he expects from his listeners. One may see this progression most clearly in such letters as Romans,
Galatians, and 1 Thessalonians. The distinctive feature of 2 Corinthians,
however, is the absence of an extended ethical section, for the focus of 2
Corinthians is the legitimacy of Paul's ministry and the restoration of reciprocal pride between Paul and this church (2 Cor 1:12–14). In 2 Corinthians
Paul's argument moves from his defense to the request for the collection
in chapters 8–9, and the argument in chapters 1–7 lays the foundation for
that request. Paul has been declaring his pride in the Corinthians and defending himself in order to restore their pride in him. In 7:4 he reaffirms
his confidence in them, and in 7:5–16 he indicates that the Corinthians
have responded appropriately to the tearful letter that he had sent to them.
In chapters 8–9 Paul again affirms his desire to boast of the Corinthians
(8:24—9:5).

At the end of 1 Corinthians (16:1–2), Paul had mentioned the collection "for the saints," indicating that he had instructed the Galatian
churches to participate also. This collection is probably the same one that
he mentions when he describes his commitment to the leaders in Jerusalem
that he and his coworkers would "remember the poor" (Gal 2:10) as they
conducted their mission to the gentiles. When Paul writes 2 Corinthians
from Macedonia (cf. 7:5), a year has passed since he first mentioned the
collection (8:10) to the Corinthians. He now reports that the Macedonians

are participating in this major project (8:2–6). Later Paul will write Romans from Corinth, declaring that "Macedonia and Achaia [i.e., Corinth] are participating in the collection for the poor among the saints in Jerusalem" (Rom 15:26). Paul has involved his gentile churches in a project that lasts several years. Therefore, he is involved in more than the disaster relief that Acts describes in 11:27–30. As Paul's comments in Romans suggests, this collection is the major work of his life. He is willing to delay his trip to Rome and risk danger in order to take this collection to Jerusalem (cf. Rom 15:30–32). Inasmuch as Paul later wrote from Corinth of the Corinthians' participation in the collection, we may assume that Paul's appeal in 2 Cor 8–9 produced the desired results.

Although Paul uses all of the resources in his rhetorical arsenal to persuade the Corinthians to participate in the collection, he never indicates in the letter precisely why this project is so important to him that it determines his travel plans. In Romans he offers a clearer picture. The churches of Macedonia and Achaia are engaged in "partnership" (κοινωνία, NRSV "share their resources") with the believers in Jerusalem. That is, the collection is an expression of the unity between gentile and Jewish churches. Furthermore, Paul knows the long-awaited expectation that the wealth of the nations will flow to Zion in the end time (cf. Isa 45:14; Isa 60:5–17; 61:6; Mic 4:13). If the Jerusalem Christians receive the collection, they will acknowledge the legitimacy of Paul's ministry among the gentiles and the unity of the church. The collection, therefore, is an expression of solidarity between the Jewish and gentile churches.

The commentaries point to several challenges in the interpretation of chapters 8 and 9. In the first place, the introduction of a new topic in 8:1 appears to be a major break in the flow of 2 Corinthians, suggesting to many commentators that 7:16 marks the end of Paul's "letter of reconciliation" (1:1—2:13 + 7:5–16). In the second place, the argument for the collection in chapter 8 is coherent in its own right and appears to be disconnected from the previous chapters. In the third place, the apparent new beginning in 9:1 ("Now it is not necessary for me to write to you about the ministry to the saints") suggests that chapter 9 is a separate letter about the collection. These anomalies have given rise to numerous attempts to partition 2 Corinthians into separate units, which one can see in the major commentaries.

Despite the literary challenges, I suggest that chapters 8 and 9 fit well with the flow of the argument. We may note, in the first place, that a major issue in both Corinthian letters is Paul's refusal to accept financial support from those who had wished to be patrons. Paul's financial independence has been a source of enmity with the Corinthians (see 2 Cor 11:7-11). In 2 Corinthians Paul is under suspicion that he has "taken advantage of" the Corinthians (cf. 7:2; 12:17). The fact that Paul is involved in collecting funds has now raised suspicions about his handling of money (cf. 8:16-24). We may note, in the second place, that chapter 8 follows easily from chapter 7. The signs of reconciliation between the Corinthians and Paul now create the conditions in which Paul can again address the topic of the collection. The fact that Titus is filled with affection for the Corinthians (cf. 7:13-16) provides a new opportunity for Titus to return to complete the collection (8:6). I suggest that chapters 8-9 are not an intrusion into Paul's argument about his ministry but rather the climax of the discussion. Paul's desire to boast about the Corinthians (1:14; 7:4) can now be illustrated in the Corinthians' response to his request for the collection (8:24—9:5).

Scholars have correctly noted that both chapters 8 and 9 can stand separately as complete arguments for the collection. However, we may also note the links that tie the two chapters together. They are bound by an inclusion that marks the beginning and end of the section on the collection. In 8:1 Paul introduces the topic of the "grace of God," while in 9:15 he speaks of God's "indescribable gift." In both instances he employs the Greek *charis* to describe the collection, not as a human activity but as God's gift. Indeed, *charis* is the dominant thread in Paul's discussion of the collection in chapters 8 and 9 (cf. 8:4, 6, 7, 9, 16, 19; 9:8, 14-15). We may note also that Paul continues discussing his desire to boast about the Corinthians to the brothers taking up the collection in 8:16-24 and 9:1-5. Thus in chapters 8 and 9 Paul makes an extended case for the Corinthians' participating in the collection, hoping to fulfill his goal of demonstrating his reconciliation with this community and to answer those who find fault with his ministry.

Although we are justified in reading chapters 8-9 as one unit, scholars who regard the two chapters as separate speeches on the collection have offered a valuable insight that will be useful for preaching. Each chapter offers a separate argument and can provide the appropriate text for preaching. Indeed, because the argument is composed of several components, the preacher may choose smaller units within this extended argument. In the lectionary, only 8:7-15 appears as a reading. As I shall indicate below, this passage is the central argument of chapter 8.

The Partnership of Giving (2 Cor 8)

If the Corinthians had not raised the issue about Paul's handling of money, he might never have made this lengthy presentation on giving. One may wonder if the fact that they provide coherent arguments apart from their presence in the letter reflects the fact that Paul is here integrating into his lessons the sermons that he has given on other occasions. The passage offers an extraordinary insight into Paul's approach to issues that confront the contemporary church, as we can see in his introduction to the topic in 8:1, "We want you to know about the grace of God that has been granted to the churches of Macedonia." Paul obviously does not treat the collection as a secular intrusion into the life of the church but as an expression of the grace of God. Elsewhere he associates God's grace with the gift of salvation (8:9; cf. Rom 3:24; 5:2, 15, 17) or with God's sustaining power for those who reach the limit of their human resources (cf. 4:15; 12:9). Just as "the grace of God" is present in human weakness, the community's handling of financial resources is also the occasion for God's grace. Indeed, as I indicated above, Paul's favorite word for the collection is *grace*.

Although Paul had earlier commanded his churches to participate in the collection (1 Cor 16:1–2), he appeals to the Corinthians in chapter 8 without ever actually commanding them to participate. Scholars have observed that chapter 8 reflects Paul's extraordinary skill as an orator as he first introduces the topic with a narrative that provides the context for Paul's appeal (8:1–7) before he presents a threefold argument for the collection. In the first place, he presents a brief argument based on the story of Christ (8:9). In the second place, he argues for the appropriateness of their participation (8:10–12). In the third place, he argues on the basis of equality (8:13–15) before he assures the listeners of his integrity (8:16–24).

The handbooks for orators recommended that the oration begin by introducing the topic in such a way as to make the audience favorably disposed toward the topic. As a skillful orator, Paul introduces the topic by offering the example of others who have demonstrated the conduct that he expects of his listeners. The Macedonians include the Philippians and Thessalonians, who demonstrate the meaning of the grace of God. Just as Paul experiences God's power in the midst of his weakness (cf. 4:7–15), their joy and the deep poverty "have overflowed in a wealth of generosity" (8:2). We can only speculate about the reason for the poverty of these churches as they live in affluent cities. The most likely cause is that they suffer the economic consequences of discrimination and harassment because of their faith (cf. Phil 1:28; 1 Thess 1:6; 2:14–16). Paul's point is not, however, the source of their hardship but the fact that they illustrate a major theme of the letter: that believers experience God's grace in the midst of weakness (cf. 12:9). One can experience wealth in the midst of poverty (cf. 6:10). In his claim that the Macedonians "gave beyond their means" (literally "beyond their power"), they illustrate Paul's frequent claim that God's power supplies the needs of the powerless. Jesus himself "was crucified in weakness, but lives by the power of God" (13:4).

When we observe that the text of 8:1–6 is all one sentence in Greek, the focus of Paul's opening words comes into view. The main clause of the sentence is 8:1, "We want you to know . . . about the grace of God that has been granted to the churches of Macedonia," followed by a series of dependent clauses that illustrate God's grace. In 8:4, Paul says that the Macedonians had been "begging earnestly" (μετὰ πολλῆς παρακλήσεως δεόμενοι) for the privilege of participating in the collection. As a result, according to 8:6, Paul is moved to "urge" (παρακαλέσαι) Titus to complete the collection at Corinth. That is, the Macedonians' urgent request to Paul leads to his urgent request to Titus to complete the collection.

Paul's language in 8:4 indicates the theological significance of the collection. One is struck by the lack of fiscal terminology in Paul's accumulation of theological words for the collection, which is not reflected well in the NRSV. The collection is literally "grace" (χάρις), "fellowship/partnership" (κοινωνία), and "ministry" (διακονία). As I have indicated above, grace is the favorite word for the collection throughout this context. Partnership (also "fellowship" in some translations) indicates the solidarity of believers with Christ (1 Cor 1:9) and with other Christians. Indeed, Paul declares in 1 Corinthians that the Lord's Supper is the "partnership" in the body and blood of Christ that creates the unity of believers (10:16–17). "Ministry" is the word that is most under dispute in 2 Corinthians (cf. 3:7–11; 4:2; 6:4; 11:23). Here, as in 9:1, Paul declares that the collection is a dimension of the ministry in which he is engaged. Thus because Paul does not separate fiscal needs from the spiritual life of his congregations, he chooses theological words to describe the collection.

The Macedonians gave generously, according to 8:5, as a demonstration of a deeper commitment: "they gave themselves first to the Lord." Thus they illustrate the larger principle of Paul's understanding of Christian existence. He expects his listeners to follow his example of finding a new identity in Christ, according to which believers present their entire existence to God, recognizing that they are "not their own" (cf. 1 Cor 6:20). Just as they "present their bodies" to Christ (Rom 12:2), they "give themselves to the Lord." Such giving has the financial consequences that Paul attributes to the Macedonians. The result of the Macedonians' eagerness to give is that Paul now urges Titus to complete "this generous undertaking" (χάρις) among the Corinthians (8:6). Having recently returned with a good report about the Corinthians, Titus is now prepared to return for unfinished business. Paul expects the Macedonian example to stimulate the Corinthians to participate.

In 8:7–15 Paul turns from the past to the future—from the Macedonian example to the Corinthians' response. Paul offers the thesis statement of the argument in v. 7 and then makes his case in vv. 7–15. Once more we see how gently Paul addresses the subject of finances at Corinth as he begins, in good oratorical style, with compliments for his readers that are intended to make them favorably disposed toward the request. We may compare Paul's gracious words in 1 Cor 1:5, which were also addressed to a troubled church. "Faith, speech, and knowledge" are common attributes of Christian communities (cf. Rom 15:14; 2 Cor 4:6; Phil 3:8; 1 Thess 3:2, 5) and of Paul himself (cf. 2 Cor 6:6). The listeners' abundance becomes the basis for the request "in order that [they] may also excel in this grace" (8:7 my translation). Paul makes no commands throughout this chapter, but gently makes a request just as he does when he asks Philemon to receive the slave Onesimus (Phlm 8–9; cf. 1 Cor 7:6). Having established their "earnestness" (σπουδή) through Titus's visit (7:12), he writes now to test the genuineness of their love "against the earnestness of others" (8:8). Thus his request is so subtle that we almost miss it. Even if the Corinthians excel in a variety of Christian attributes, they are incomplete unless they, like the Macedonians, excel in the grace of giving. He hopes that his love for them (8:7) will motivate them to give as he tests the genuineness of their love (8:8).

Paul introduces his most powerful argument for the collection in 8:9. The ultimate act of grace (NRSV "generous act") was the gift of Jesus Christ for the people: "though he was rich, yet for your sakes he became poor, so that by his poverty you might become rich." Paul is probably referring to a confessional statement that the Corinthians already know, appealing to the common ground that he shares with the Corinthians. Paul commonly appeals to the story of Jesus in order to shape the values of his congregations. In Philippians he appeals for harmony within the church, recalling that Christ was first "in the form of God" before he "emptied himself" and "humbled himself" at the cross. In describing Jesus' descent from wealth to poverty, Paul is telling the story of the incarnation, as he did in Philippians. Thus the Christian faith began with this extraordinary grace, which should now determine the conduct of the Corinthians. Just as the story of Christ's incarnation shapes the ethical response of Christians in general, it shapes the Corinthians' attitude toward giving. Thus sacrificial giving is nothing less than a participation in grace.

In vv. 10–12 Paul presents the second argument for participation in the collection, urging the Corinthians to let their earlier intention become a reality. Here Paul argues from the appropriateness of participating in the collection. Once more, he chooses to give advice (cf. 1 Cor 7:25, 40) rather than to command. He reminds them that God's acceptance is based on what they have rather than on what they do not have (8:10–12).

In the third argument he concludes with the equality of the communities (8:13–15). In describing the "acceptable" gift, he recalls Israel's sacrifices, according to which they presented offerings that were "acceptable" to God (cf. Rom 15:16). In his call for equality (8:13), he recalls Israel's experience of the manna in the wilderness when "The one who had much did not have too much, and the one who had little did not have too little" (8:15; cf. Exod 16:18). Like Israel, the church is composed of a community that is genuine only insofar as those who are affluent share their gifts with those who are less affluent. Paul envisions a Christian solidarity between his churches that is not limited to words alone but consists of the sharing of possessions.

Before proceeding to a new argument in chapter 9, Paul pauses to reassure the Corinthians of his integrity in collecting the funds. Indeed, the striking fact about Paul's project is that he does not collect the funds at all. In 8:16–24 he mentions three men who have impeccable credentials for the task. Titus (8:16–17) has the full trust of the Corinthians. Paul sends with him a brother who has been "appointed by the churches" (8:19) and another brother whom Paul has tested many times (8:22). They are not only Paul's emissaries; the unnamed men are "messengers of the churches" (8:23). Some scholars have suggested that the long list of names of Paul's companions in Acts 20:4–5 includes these and other messengers of the churches. We do not know why Paul does not name these brothers, and it is useless to speculate. The point is that Paul anticipates the suspicions surrounding his handling of money, and he chooses to use people of impeccable reputation to ensure that no one find fault with his ministry (8:20; cf. 6:3–4). The collection is so important that he does not want it undermined by the mere appearance of impropriety.

Reflections for Preaching and Teaching (2 Cor 8)

The fact that this detailed argument addresses a perennial issue in the life of the church provides our hermeneutical entry into the text. Church leaders, like Paul, must respond to the multiple criticisms of the church in its relationship to money. Much of this criticism is well deserved. Parachurch organizations sometimes spend an inordinate amount of their gifts on fundraising. Churches sometimes raise funds that benefit themselves rather than those who need their gifts most. The recreation center for the church's youth may have more support than the contribution to alleviate hunger in the drought-stricken developing world. The church often does not exercise sufficient transparency to ensure the trust of its givers. Because of this cynicism, we may be reticent to talk much about financial commitments for fear of alienating our congregations. I suggest that we have here a point of contact with Paul's situation and a basis for our reflection on the relationship between our Christian commitment and our finances.

Preacher should note that Paul's request for funds is not a matter of meeting the church's deficit or remodeling its building. Paul has a specific goal, about which he has already instructed the congregation: the solidarity of rich and poor churches. Thus he is totally unembarrassed to talk about money. Paul can serve as a model for us only insofar as our requests are worthy of sacrifice, that is, if they benefit others in a concrete way. Any sermon on giving must indicate clearly how such sacrifice fulfills the mission of the church.

Because chapter 8 is a coherent rhetorical unit, we may preach the entire passage, following the sequence of Paul's argument and drawing parallels to our own situation. As we follow Paul's argument, we may offer examples of other "Macedonians" in the recent past who have demonstrated such generosity that they have stimulated us to give. In keeping with Paul's argument, we may remind the church that the incarnation is the one gift that shapes the minds of all believers. Recipients of such an extraordinary gift become engaged in acts of giving to others. Then we follow the remainder of Paul's argument, indicating that the Christian understanding of equality is not only a spiritual matter but involves solidarity across economic lines and our integrity in handling the funds.

Because this passage is long and dense, we may choose specific units within the sermon. One may, for example, limit the sermon to 8:1–9. Here we can focus on the theological dimension to our finances (8:4), indicating that the Macedonians were engaged in "grace, fellowship, and ministry." These words, all of which refer to the larger Christian story, also refer to the use of funds. Thus our giving is a vital component of our larger ministry. The sermon could move toward the incarnation as the event that shaped the Christian attitude toward selflessness. The second option is to follow the lectionary, using 8:7–15 as the basis for the sermon. As the central argument for giving, this text begins with the request and then offers three arguments for the collection. A third option is to focus on 8:16–24 and the need for the church to be irreproachable in its handling of money. We could begin with the cynicism that surrounds the church and then show that Paul provides a model of conduct that is honorable in the sight of others (8:21).

The Blessings of Giving (2 Cor 9)

In chapter 9 Paul's argument for the collection is both a continuation of the preceding argument and a new direction in the argument. The connection with chapter 8 is evident in Paul's claim that he boasts of the Corinthians to the churches and in the hope he expressed in 9:1–5 that his boasts will not lead to his embarrassment. Paul also continues to discuss the role of the brothers in 9:1–5 after introducing them in 8:16–24. At the same time, the opening words of chapter 9, "Now it is not necessary for me to write you about the ministry to the saints," marks a new beginning. We need not conclude, as many scholars do, that Paul wrote chapter 9 independently of chapter 8 since the discussion in chapter 9 reflects the same stage in Paul's attempt to ensure the Corinthians' participation in the collection. A year has passed since Paul began that project with the Corinthians (8:10; 9:2). Nevertheless, despite the links with chapter 8, chapter 9 offers a new argument for the collection.

Once more we observe Paul's careful rhetorical strategy. In 9:1–5 he begins to build his case, offering the background for the request and describing his present situation as he sends the brothers to receive the collection. Verse 6 is the thesis statement of the argument for generosity. He offers a general principle of the benefits of generosity and then develops this theme in vv. 7–15.

Having observed Paul's argument in chapter 8, we are immediately surprised as Paul lays the foundation for the new argument in 9:1–5. Paul has boasted to the Corinthians about the Macedonians in 8:1–6, and now he tells the Corinthians that he is boasting about them to the Macedonians (9:2). Moreover, the boast that "Achaia has been ready since last year" (9:2) appears to conflict directly with Paul's earlier encouragement to the Corinthians to complete what they began "last year" (8:10). While Paul's claim that the Corinthians have had the "eagerness" (προθυμία) for a year is consistent with 8:10–12, his claim that they have been ready for that length of time is an example of Paul's rhetorical tactic, for his fear of being embarrassed indicates his concern about the Corinthians' readiness. Here, as in 8:7, Paul's purpose is to make the listeners favorably disposed toward the request that follows. In his claim that he boasts about the Corinthians, he continues a theme of the letter (1:14; 7:4) that he reiterated in 8:24: his boasting about them in the churches. We must not miss the rhetorical point. Paul is the anxious parent who places the Corinthians' conduct in the most favorable light in order to say, "Do not let me down. I am counting on you."

Paul also wants the Corinthians to see the collection in the proper light. As in chapter 8, he employs theological language to describe it. According to 9:1, it is "the ministry to the saints" (cf. 8:4). According to 9:5, it is a "blessing" (εὐλογία; NRSV renders "voluntary gift") rather than an extortion (πλεονεξία). Paul knows that all blessings come from God in abundance (cf. Rom 15:29; Gal 3:14; Heb 6:7). To participate in the collection, therefore, is to share in the bounty of what God is doing.

Having described the current situation in 9:1–5, Paul makes his case in 9:6–15, beginning with the thesis statement in 9:6: "The one who sows sparingly will reap sparingly, and the one who sows bountifully will reap bountifully." That one reaps what one sows is a truism that ancient people applied metaphorically to a number of circumstances (cf. Ps 126:5–6). Paul applies this saying in his argument with the Galatians (6:7–8). Here he shifts the focus to an emphasis on the generosity of our sowing, the abundance of the harvest, and the cheerfulness of our giving (9:7). The remainder of the argument indicates the blessings that accompany giving.

In the first place, Paul emphasizes the blessings to the giver. In 9:8–10 he explains this harvest, again equating the church's experience with that of Israel (cf. 8:15; Exod 16:18) and placing the focus on the power of God. The phrase "God is able to multiply" employs the verb δυνατεῖ, which may also be translated "God has the power." The consistent emphasis of the book is the conviction that God's power (δύναμις) is present in human weakness (cf. 1:8; 4:7; 6:7; 8:3; 13:4). God's power was present in human weakness at the cross and resurrection of Christ (13:3), and it continues to empower the servants of Christ (cf. 4:7). Here Paul claims that God can take meager funds and multiply them. In 9:9 Paul appeals to Psalm 112:9, a passage that originally spoke of the lasting results of those who give to the poor. Paul makes God the subject of the sentence, indicating that the community's gifts are actually the work of God, whose righteousness lives on through the gifts of the people.

Paul's suggestion that the believer actually benefits from giving is not to be understood as an early form of the gospel of wealth, for he makes no claim that believers are financially enriched by their giving. Instead, he offers the promise that they will have "enough of everything" so that they may abound "in every good work" (9:5). The word "enough" (αὐτάρκεια) is used in relation to money also in Phil 4:11, where Paul is an example of the outlook that he expects of his churches. He has learned to be "content" (αὐτάρκης) with whatever he has (4:11). One may compare the reflections on wealth in 1 Tim 6:6, in which there is great gain in "godliness with contentment" (αὐτάρκεια). The ancient Stoics advocated the simple life unencumbered by possessions and held this virtue of contentment in especially high regard. Paul employs this language to emphasize that God will not abandon givers who exhaust themselves. Indeed, just as God's presence "abounds" in our weakness (cf. 1:5; 4:15; 8:2), believers "share abundantly in every good work" (9:8) because of the continuing grace of God.

In the second place, Paul insists that Christian giving results in thanksgiving and glory to God. Paul uses the language of sacrifice to describe the offering as the "ministry of this service" (διακονία τῆς λειτουργίας ταύτης, NRSV "rendering of this service"). Paul applies the language of λειτουργία to his own work (cf. Rom 15:16; Phil 2:17) and to others who devote themselves to the service of God (cf. Phil 2:30). Christian gifts are, therefore, a "priestly service" to God. Consequently, Paul says that their gifts result in thanksgiving and glory to God (9:12, 13).

In the third place, Christian gifts benefit the recipients and create the ties of solidarity between them and the givers. They supply a need (9:12), and they create the ties of "partnership" (κοινωνία, 9:13; cf. 8:4) among believers. As a result, the believers "long for you and pray for you" in ties that transcend regional borders.

Reflections for Preaching and Teaching (2 Cor 9)

If, as I mentioned above, we are reticent to preach from texts on giving because of the distortions of this theme and the resulting cynicism, this passage is especially problematic inasmuch as it sounds dangerously like the word of the televangelist who promises that financial support is a better investment than blue chip stock. If the focus of the sermon is rooted in the text's center of gravity, we must reflect on Paul's promise that one who gives generously will receive a blessing. We must, on the one hand, ask if this promise rings true for us. As we appropriate this text, we should regard Paul's promise not as an axiom that is true under all circumstances but as an argument that fits within the wisdom tradition. This argument reflects the common experience of the faithful more than an objective fact. On the other hand, we must ask if Paul has appealed to our selfish instincts in his promise that giving will result in greater blessings.

Since this is a troublesome text, I suggest that this question provides our point of entry into the sermon. An appropriate introduction to the sermon is to confront the question and the claim that giving results in the increase of our financial well-being. We may offer examples of those who treat Paul's statement in 9:6 as the offer of increased wealth for the giver. The sermon may then answer this question.

We may first concede the fundamental principle that God's power is present in our weakness. If indeed God is present in our weakness, we can believe that God can use our resources and multiply them, for the essence of faith is to trust that God provides. Thus in a sense, we can believe that God benefits those who give.

God's blessings do not involve increased wealth, however, but *enough*. We will do well to know what *enough* really is. The mark of our affluent society is that we really do not know what *enough* means. While we consume more than our share of the world's resources, we turn a blind eye to malnutrition and hopelessness. God does not promise increased wealth but *enough*—enough for "every good work."

Our giving to others is, in fact, our sacrifice to God and a means of showing solidarity with others. We give, not in order to enrich ourselves, but to participate in God's work of giving. We do not, like the Macedonians, give out of our poverty. We take the risk of giving to others out of the extraordinary wealth, joining others who have recognized the extraordinary wealth of knowing that they have "enough."

Chapter 5

THE FINAL APPEAL

2 Corinthians 10–13

A COMMON FEATURE OF Paul's letters is his preparation for a future visit when he will renew his relationship to the community from which he is separated (cf. 1 Cor 4:14–21; Phil 2:19–25; Rom 15:22–29; 1 Thess 3:11–14; Phlm 22). In 2 Cor 10–13 Paul's impending visit forms the background and frame for his final appeal for reconciliation. In 10:2 he anticipates his future presence with the Corinthians, and in 12:14 he mentions the upcoming third visit to the Corinthians. Finally, he mentions the third visit again in 13:1–4. Such visits can be the occasion for a happy reunion, as Paul suggests in other letters (cf. Phil 2:19–30; Phlm 22), or they can be the occasion when the parent chastises the child (cf. 1 Cor 4:14–21). Paul obviously anticipates the third visit with considerable foreboding as he recalls the disaster of his second visit (2:1–4) and expresses uncertainty in chapters 1–9 whether the Corinthians will reciprocate his devotion and boasting on their behalf (cf. 6:11–13; 7:2–4). Thus in each reference to his visit in 2 Corinthians, he announces his visit with either a threat (10:2; 13:1) or a continuation of the argument of the earlier part of the letter (12:14).

When we recall that letters were actually sermons read orally, we are amazed at the change of tone between 9:15 and 10:1, where Paul moves from an expression of gratitude to the resumption of his defense. Since chapters 10–13 contain a coherent and sometimes bitter argument, many interpreters conclude that this section comes from a different time in Paul's relationship with the Corinthians and that it did not belong originally with all of chapters 1–9, as I have pointed out in the introduction. Some hold that chapters 10–13 come from a period prior to chapters 1–9 and that they may in fact contain the "tearful letter" described in 2:1–4. Others argue that chapters 10–13 come from a later stage in Paul's relationship to the Corinthians. However, since a final warning is not uncommon in Paul's letters (cf. Rom 16:17-20; 1 Cor 16:21; Gal 6:11–17), we should not be surprised to find one here. Furthermore, while Paul speaks with greater intensity in chapters 10–13 than in the earlier chapters, he has already introduced these themes indirectly. As in chapters 1–9 the issue is the legitimacy of his ministry. Paul has already distinguished himself from the "peddlers" (2:17) and from those who commend themselves through letters (3:1–3), and now he continues these themes.

Ancient rhetorical theorists described the conclusion of the speech (*peroratio*) as the occasion for summarizing the argument with special *pathos*. The speakers could defend themselves and blame others while addressing the issues under dispute. I suggest that chapters 10–13 are actually the *peroratio* of 2 Corinthians. Paul speaks directly to issues that he has addressed only indirectly before. In this section we learn more about the opponents and their charges against Paul than we have learned thus far. Thus the letter is an appropriate conclusion to Paul's defense of his conduct. He has begged the Corinthians to accept his ministry in chapters 1–9; now, with special vehemence, he demands their response.

True and False Boasting (2 Cor 10:1–18)

A War of Ideas (2 Cor 10:1–11)

Since Paul rarely mentions himself by name (cf. Gal 5:2), the introduction, "I Paul myself" (or "I and no one else"), is noteworthy as a signal for the intensity of his response. At the beginning and end of 10:1–11, Paul indicates the nature of the charges against him. In 10:2 he refers to their charges when he says, "I who am humble when present and bold when I am absent." In 10:10 he refers again to their charges: "They say that his letters are weighty and strong, but his presence of body is weak and his speech is of no account" (10:10). The charges reflect the values of Greek culture, according to which Paul did not measure up to common expectations. Humility, for example, was associated with servility and humiliation, as in Paul's description of his choice of working with his hands: "Did I commit a sin when

I humbled myself?" (11:7). Courage was one of the four cardinal virtues in Greek thought, and its opposite was humility. The ideal philosopher, according to Greek thought, spoke with frankness and was confident in himself. The Greeks ridiculed the stock character of the flatterer, who was both humble and weak, while they admired the one who possessed physical strength, courage, and presence. Thus the opponents' charges against Paul indicate that they measured him by the standards of Greek thought, arguing that, while he wrote strong letters, he showed no courage in their midst.

The focal point of Paul's response to these criticisms is his insistence in 10:2 that he stands ready to demonstrate the courage and authority that they question. One may not measure this authority, however, by the standards of Greek culture, for Paul appeals to his listeners "by the meekness and gentleness of Christ" (10:1). Just as he finds his identity in the crucified Christ (cf. 4:10), he points to the humility and weakness that his opponents disdain as the sign of his apostolic ministry. Paul's request not to have to be bold (10:2), like his threat in 13:1, indicates the nature of his courage. Contrary to those who suppose that he conducts himself according to human standards (10:2, κατὰ σάρκα, literally "according to the flesh"; cf. 5:16), he is actually engaged in a military campaign that corresponds to divine standards. According to the values of God's world, he is not weak, but has weapons that are mighty for the tearing down of strongholds." He does not conduct his military campaign against literal armies; he tears down arguments and brings every thought captive to Christ. In response to the charges of his weakness, he portrays himself as the leader of a military unit that will tear down enemy fortresses.

In this extended military metaphor, Paul follows the philosophers who regularly spoke of the battle for the mind in which they were engaged. Epictetus, for example, said that the philosopher's authority does not derive from weapons and bodyguards but from his conscience and a purified mind (*Diss.* 3.22.13–19). Paul's near contemporary Philo described the fortresses as the diversions of the mind that must be destroyed (Cf. *Conf.* 128–31). Like the philosophers, Paul is engaged in the battle with bad ideas, and he will demonstrate his courage as he destroys the bad ideas of his opponents. Like the prophets before him, he has the authority to build and not to tear down (10:8; cf. Jer 24:6), which they will see on his next visit if they do not respond appropriately to his message.

Reflections for Preaching and Teaching (2 Cor 10:1–11)

Our hermeneutical task is to make the transition between Paul's argument and our own situation. Because Paul is describing his apostolic authority, we cannot identify with him. I suggest that we identify with the Corinthians, conceding that we reflect many of the same cultural values that were at stake in Paul's argument with them. In Paul we hear a voice that confronts us with the challenge to see the world with the new eyes that come from the crucified Christ and to recognize that we are involved in a battle of ideas between the Christian revelation and our own values of strength and weakness. This passage challenges our natural ways of measuring leadership and the church's mission.

This passage, like others in 2 Corinthians, is likely to meet a negative response in our congregations. Paul's military metaphors may offend our deep desire to avoid conflict. His sharp distinction between the good ideas of divine revelation and the bad ideas of human culture are also troublesome to a culture that prefers tolerance over the claims for truth. The preacher may choose, therefore, to begin by engaging these issues, asking the listeners if they are troubled by Paul's call for the conflict against bad ideas, some of which invade the church. Then one may indicate what was at stake for Paul: the encroachment of bad ideas into the church would destroy his work. The Christian community was called into being by the claim that God has imparted divine insight through the crucified Christ. To measure people according to their physical status, as in Corinth, is not compatible with the "meekness and gentleness of Christ." The church has engaged in a battle against materialism and racism, for example, and it continues to be challenged by ideas that undermine the Christian faith. Our passage is not, however, an invitation to turn disagreements within the church into hostilities. It challenges us to examine ideas in light of the gospel of the crucified Lord.

Boasting in the Lord (2 Cor 10:12–18)

In 10:12–18 the triangular relationship between Paul, the Corinthians, and "some" (10:2, 12; cf. 10:10, "they say") forms the link with 10:1–11. While in 10:2, 10 Paul reports what his opponents are saying about him, in the new unit he speaks ironically, saying "We do not dare to classify ourselves with some of those who commend themselves." In the words "we do not dare" (οὐ γὰρ τολμῶμεν, 10:12) he refers to the questions about his courage in 10:1–2, indicating that he chooses not to engage in the same kind of self-promotion that characterizes the opponents. The context in 10:1–11 suggests that the opponents compare their own courage, physical presence, and eloquence favorably with Paul's public persona. Paul's statement that they "compare themselves" and "commend themselves" (10:12) provides insight into a constant theme of the letter that is unique to 2 Corinthians. Paul's earlier references to self-commendation (cf. 3:1; 4:2; 5:12; 6:4) are a response to the opponents' own boasting. Indeed, in chapters 10–13 Paul uses forms of the word "boast" (καυχ-) eighteen times in response to opponents who "boast according to human standards" (11:18). Paul engages in the extended "fool's speech," the centerpiece of chapters 10–13, boasting of his own struggles (11:1—12:13), and concluding, "You forced me to do it. Indeed, you should have been the ones commending me" (12:11). Paul introduces this "fool's speech" in 10:12–18, indicating that he rejects the opponents' practice of self-comparison.

The self-comparison in which Paul's opponents were engaged was a basic tool of ancient orators. In the second century CE Lucian said, "If anyone accosts you, make marvelous assertions about yourself, and be extravagant in your self-praise." However, others argued against this practice. Aristotle said, "To speak at great length about oneself, and to make all kinds of professions; and to take the credit for what another has done . . . this is a sign of pretentiousness."[1] Because self-praise had to be handled delicately, Plutarch wrote the essay "On Praising Oneself Inoffensively," in which he indicated the circumstances in which one might praise oneself. Self-praise is inoffensive, according to Plutarch, when we have some other end in view. "Consider first, then, whether a man might praise himself to exhort his hearers and inspire them with emulation and ambition, as Nestor by recounting his own exploits and battles incited Patroclus and roused the nine champions to offer themselves for the single combat" (*Mor.* 544). It is also appropriate when one also adds to the points of praise minor shortcomings or faults. One may also engage in self-praise in order to defend oneself against attacks made by opponents.

In 10:12 Paul rejects the opponents' practice of comparing themselves with others and then clarifies his approach in 10:13–16. The passage is notoriously difficult in Greek, as Paul says literally, "We will not boast beyond measure, but according to the measure of the canon (κανών)

---

1. Lucian, "A Professor of Public Speaking," 13.21; Aristotle, *Rhet.* 2.6.11–12.

which God has apportioned." The NRSV and NIV render κανών as "field" of endeavor (10:13, 15). Paul is apparently referring to his mission field as an endeavor in which he stayed within the limits determined by God. He came to the Corinthians because he was commissioned and empowered by God. Despite the obscurity of the passage, Paul's point appears to be clear. His repeated use of the negative in verses 13–15 indicates that he knew his limitations and refused to boast "beyond limits," unlike the opponents, whose boasts reflect their arrogance. He desires only to see the growth in the Corinthians' faith (10:15), hoping to extend his work beyond them in the future (10:16).

Before Paul begins the "fool's speech," in which he matches the opponents' boasting (cf. 11:18–22), he places all boasting in perspective: "Let the one who boasts, boast in the Lord" (10:17). Here Paul quotes the words of Jer 9:23, which he had also cited to the pretentious listeners of 1 Corinthians (1:31). Unlike the opponents, who boast of their achievements, Paul limits his boast to work that God has given him (10:13–16). When he engages in boasting in chapter 11, he recognizes that God is the one who has empowered him for service.

Reflections for Preaching and Teaching (2 Cor 10:12–18)

The focus of this passage is its challenge to the hubris that recognizes no limits to human achievement. We lived through most of the twentieth century with amazing successes in science and technology that led us to believe that we knew no limits in human achievement. Progress in communications, travel, health care, and human comforts appeared to be unlimited until the latter part of the twentieth century, when we discovered our own limitations. We could not continue to consume more energy, build bigger cities, conquer more diseases, and add to our comforts without paying a price. Recent changes have affected our self-confidence as a culture as we have seen our limits.

Paul's recognition of the limits set by God is a challenge to our corporate self-confidence. We assume that we can apply our human ingenuity to solve the problems that face the church. The sermon may find its point of contact in our identification with the opponents, who trusted in themselves. Then it may move toward Paul's conclusion: Our only boasts are in what God does in our midst.

The Fool's Speech (2 Cor 11:1—12:13)

In the "fool's speech" in 11:1—12:13, Paul offers his credentials as a minister, boasting of the activities that legitimize his claim to the loyalty of the Corinthians and making the final defense of his ministry. At the beginning and the end of this speech, Paul acknowledges that such boasting is foolish (11:1; 12:11; cf. 11:21, 23), but indicates that the Corinthians have forced him into the practice by listening to the boasts of the rival missionaries (12:11). In chapter 10 Paul had prepared the way for the fool's speech by describing the challenges to his ministry by the opponents. They had compared themselves to Paul (10:12), criticizing him for his weakness, poor speech, and humility, suggesting that Paul's weak persona and lack of courage were evidence that he was not a man of the Spirit (10:1–11). Paul responded with reflections on proper boasting in 10:12–18 before beginning his actual boasting in the fool's speech in chapter 11.

The Prologue (2 Cor 11:1–21)

Since Paul's boasting actually begins in 11:22 and concludes in 12:10, the body of the fool's speech includes 11:22—12:10. In 12:11-13 Paul summarizes the speech. He sets the stage for the fool's speech with a prologue in 11:1-21, indicating what is at stake in the boasting that follows. In the inclusion of 11:1, 21, we see what is at stake. In 11:20-21 Paul accuses the Corinthians of "putting up with" (ἀνέχω) opponents who are so overbearing that "they slap you in the face." With irony he says, "We were too weak for that." This problem is the background for 11:1, where Paul asks the Corinthians to "bear with" him (ἀνέχω). That is, if they "bear with" those who have an excess of courage (11:21; cf. 11:4, "you submit [ἀνέχω] readily enough"), perhaps they will "bear with" him. This entire section is filled with references to the dangers threatening the church.

These dangers are especially threatening insofar as Paul has a special relationship to them. As the founder of the church, he was the father of the bride who "betrothed" them to Christ and hopes to present them ultimately at the wedding to the bridegroom (11:2). Paul actually "betrothed" them at their conversion. He knows, however, that their conversion is the beginning of a corporate narrative that ends only at the coming of Christ (cf. 1:14). Earlier in the letter he has described the Holy Spirit as the "first installment" (ἀρραβών, 1:22; 5:5) of their future hope. That is, the church is unfinished business. In this triangular relationship, Paul fears that their minds will be taken captive (cf. 10:3–6). In v. 4 Paul indicates hypothetical problems. Despite the arguments of some commentators, we need not conclude that the opponents actually teach "another Jesus" or "another Spirit." Paul is expressing his concern for their openness to dangerous ideas. Paul offers an example in 11:5–6, recalling the criticism mentioned in 10:10–11. Their relationship to the opponents endangers the final outcome of their story.

In 11:7–11 he refers to one dimension of the "humility" that offends the Corinthians. He has "humbled" himself by working with his hands, refusing to allow the wealthy members to act as his patrons. He placed himself in the lowest social class, making access to the higher social classes impossible. His work with the hands was demeaning for itinerant philosophers in a world in which manual labor was often despised. Apparently, the opponents have no such qualms. They demonstrate their "courage" in their demands on the Corinthians as they "make slaves," "prey upon," and "take advantage" of them (11:20). This problem is exacerbated by the fact that other churches had supported Paul. Thus the Corinthians have accused Paul of refusing their friendship, charging him with not loving them (11:11).

Paul's debate with the opponents echoes the disputes among philosophers over the issue of the proper means for the philosopher to earn a living. Socrates, who refused to accept pay for his work, accused the Sophists of being "merchants" of their teachings rather than pursuing the truth. Earlier in 2 Corinthians Paul uses the same metaphor when he distinguishes himself from the "peddlers" of God's word (2 Cor 2:17). Here he must defend himself and demonstrate that he was acting from love. His refusal was actually an act of love, a desire not to be a burden. Indeed, as he indicates earlier in 1 Corinthians, his refusal to accept payment was his way of being shaped by the cross of Christ (1 Cor 4:11–12). He chooses to exhaust himself for others (cf. 12:14–15) rather than allow them to exhaust themselves for him.

In 11:12–21 Paul leads up to the actual fool's speech with a clear description of the specific dangers to his own work of bringing the Corinthians to maturity. The distinguishing feature of the opponents is the boasting through which they make their claim to be apostles (11:13). Because they boast by human standards, they have forced Paul into matching their boasts (11:22, 18, 21). Thus Paul responds with his own boasts in 11:22—12:10

because the Corinthians' openness to the opponents has forced him to offer his own credentials for ministry.

Reflections for Preaching and Teaching (2 Cor 11:1–21)

The focus of 11:1–21 is the church's vulnerability to the bad ideas that Paul mentioned in 10:3–4. Since this unit is the prologue to the actual "fool's speech," we face decisions about preaching texts. I suggest two different possibilities.

Option 1. One can preach from 11:1–21 while giving special emphasis to 11:1–6. Indeed, the thesis statement of this unit is 11:2–3, and the remainder of the unit is an elaboration of this statement. This unit provides a picture of a church that lives a narrative existence between its excellent beginning and its desired outcome but must survive the temptations that threaten the outcome. His church was vulnerable to the claims of those who measured ministry by the Greco-Roman standards of power and status. We may recall the vulnerabilities of the contemporary church to the spirit of our own age and recognize that we have an unfinished story. We recall numerous threats that have endangered the church: the German Christians who adapted their faith to the ideology of the Third Reich, the adaptation of our Christianity to the gospel of success and wealth, or the adaptation of the gospel to nationalism.

A focus on great beginnings is an appropriate introduction. Paul speaks of the excitement of the engagement to be married. For others it is the wedding or the birth of children. Just as we know that these are only beginnings, we know that the people of faith have only begun. Consequently, we address our vulnerability to the bad ideas of our own time, many of which masquerade as legitimate expressions of Christian faith. Our passage challenges us to recognize our temptations and to recall the countercultural nature of the cross.

Option 2. One can focus on 11:7–11. Paul's refusal to accept money for his work confronted the Greco-Roman values of money and status. Like the Corinthians, we measure our value in terms of the "net worth" measured by bank accounts or our place in the corporate pyramid. In contrast to those who would demand so much, Paul chooses not to be a burden, choosing instead to exhaust himself for others. He gives an extended explanation in 12:14–15. He challenges our understanding of possession, work, and status. Behind this explanation is a theology of the cross in which we see the value of living for others. We might imagine a community with a countercultural view of money. Our capacity to address the issues of world hunger or poverty within our own neighborhoods grows out of a transformed view of possessions.

Boasting in Weakness (2 Cor 11:22–33)

Having been forced into comparative boasting by his opponents (cf. 10:12; 11:12, 17), Paul begins his actual boasting in 11:22. Inasmuch as the entire epistle is a defense of Paul's ministry, this "fool's speech" is the climax of the letter in which Paul incorporates and expands earlier parts of the letter (cf. 4:7–15; 6:4–10). Scholars debate whether Paul is actually matching his opponents' claims or offering a parody of the catalog of adversities that were common among the philosophers. Paul is probably taking the claims of the opponents and arguing that he has done even more. He is also reframing the customary list by offering these achievements as examples of his weakness (11:29–30).

From this list we realize how little we actually know about Paul from his letters and from Acts. Most of the incidents that he describes here are unknown to us. Indeed, we would not know this information about Paul if the opponents had not forced him to describe the struggles of his ministry. The introduction in 11:21 offers a significant insight into the significance of this list for Paul. He begins, "But whatever anyone dares to boast of . . . I also dare to boast of that." The use of the word "dare" is especially significant in light of the charge that Paul is lacking in courage. He uses the same word earlier in describing the opponents' comparisons with his own personal weakness (τολμάω, 10:2, 12). Here he will finally show a side that he has not shown before. He offers the list as an indication of his daring.

In the opening triad, Paul matches his opponents' claim to Jewishness. His earlier argument (3:1–18) suggests that he is responding to Jewish opponents. His interest in triads is evident in 11:22. "Hebrew, Israelite, seed of Abraham" are overlapping categories. In a time when Jews maintained their Jewish identity in varying degrees, Paul asserts that his Jewish practice is as evident as theirs. Probably he maintains that he has kept the ancestral language and practices.

In v. 23 the phrase "Are they servants of Christ?" is the heading for the remainder of the list. The entire letter has focused on Paul's ministry (διακονία, 3:7, 9; 4:1; 5:18; 6:3; 8:4; 11:8). He moves from the claim "So am I" in reference to his Jewishness (11:22) to the claim that he is a "better" minister (11:23) and offers as evidence the following list. In vv. 23–26 his speech is characterized by the use of the comparatives and by specific numbers, which are intended to elaborate on how he is "better." Whatever the opponents have done, he has done more. The specifics here reiterate what he said in 6:4–10. Whereas he mentioned his labors, imprisonments, and floggings in 6:4, here he adds the words "far greater," "far more," and "countless."

In vv. 24–25 he mentions events otherwise unknown to the Corinthians and to us, and he supplies the actual number of occasions. The "forty lashes minus one" is a Jewish punishment (cf. Deut 25:3). The beating with rods was a common punishment given by Roman magistrates (cf. Acts 16:22). Stoning was both the Jewish means of execution and a spontaneous reaction from an angry mob (cf. Acts 14:19). Paul's travel by sea could result in shipwreck and the resulting perils of "a night and day . . . adrift at sea."

Verse 26 speaks of the difficulty of travel, mentioning the word "danger" eight times. Paul mentions the full range of travels, each of which had its own dangers. Travel in the ancient world was treacherous, as Paul indicates. He arranges the dangers into contrasting pairs: danger on land ("frequent journeys" refers to land travel) and the danger of rivers, the danger from his own countrymen and the danger from gentiles; the danger in the city and the danger in the country.

Verse 27 describes the deprivations associated with his work (cf. 6:4). As an itinerant craftsman Paul had no regular clientele for his work. The "toil and hardship" (cf. 1 Thess 2:9) of physical labor accompanied his missionary work. "Sleepless nights," hunger, and exposure to the elements were the problems associated with his difficult physical work. His constant travels resulted in a lack of regular income (cf. Phil 4:10–20).

Verse 28 adds his anxiety for the churches. Although in other contexts Paul can call on his readers to have no worries (cf. Phil 4:6), Paul is the pastor who is often in anguish about the condition of his churches, as he has indicated already in this letter (2:12–13; 7:2–4). His letter-writing activity is an indication of his care for his churches, for he is not the evangelist who plants churches and leaves them. He is, as he indicated in 11:2, the father of the bride who remains anxious until the day of the wedding.

In vv. 29–30 Paul's summation offers his interpretation of this list. All of these adversities are signs of weakness. Indeed, according to verse 30, he will boast in his weaknesses. Having begun with the claim to be daring (11:21), he reaches the conclusion of this section with the claim of weakness—the very quality for which he is criticized (cf. 10:10–11). Here Paul parts company with his opponents, who boast to demonstrate their courage in adversity. Paul's focus on God's power in the context of his weakness is a constant thread throughout the letter (cf. 4:7; 12:5, 9, 10; 13:4). In keeping with his claim that the cross was the ultimate sign of weakness (13:4), Paul does not hesitate to boast of his weaknesses, knowing that God's power is present in human weakness.

In 11:31–33 he recalls a specific story that is also known from the book of Acts (9:24–25) as an example of his weakness. When Aretas the ethnarch guarded the city in order to seize him, Paul escaped by being let down in a basket. One may check the commentaries to learn of the problems associated with this story. We do not know, for example, when Paul overlapped with Aretas in Damascus or what authority Aretas would have had. Nevertheless, we see what this story means to Paul. This occasion was such a sign of weakness that Paul would have been the subject of ridicule. Some scholars have suggested that Paul tells this story because the readers would know that high military honors were given to soldiers who were the first over the fortified city wall in times of war. Paul may be giving a parody of this practice, offering this story as a supreme example of his weakness. The story epitomizes Paul's constant claim that God provides a rescue for him in his weakness.

Reflections for Preaching (2 Cor 11:23–33)

The starting point for preaching this passage is to recognize that Paul is reluctantly offering his credentials by subverting the values of his time. The climax of Paul's list of adversities and the center of gravity for the passage is 11:29–33, where he categorizes them as weaknesses. Our task is to recognize the point of contact between the conversation in 2 Corinthians and those that occur in our own churches. Paul's message is consistent with his earlier claims that Christian faith is an expression of the continuing drama of the cross and resurrection—of power in the context of weakness. We continue to encounter Christian claims to victorious living without the weakness of the cross.

I suggest that we may find one point of entry with reflections on passages that offer a reassuring and victorious understanding of the Christian faith. Paul's words in Philippians can be reduced to bumper stickers: "Do not worry about anything, but . . . make your requests known to God" (Phil 4:6); "I can do all things through Christ who strengthens me" (Phil 4:13). Such passages resonate well for us, and we do not doubt that they are true.

This point of entry may serve as the introduction to a sermon in which we proceed to show that they were spoken to people in despair. We move now to reflect on the fact that Paul also spoke to those who were boastful in their claims in 2 Corinthians. Here he offered his credentials, indicating that he found much to worry about, for his Christian existence involved sharing a cross. Here Paul's rhetoric is so powerful that we want the congregation to hear the words of 2 Cor 11:22–33 and experience Paul's struggle.

We conclude with a return to Paul's claim of power. This power was not merely something extra for those who already live satisfied lives. God's strengthening presence comes to the Christian community when we exhaust ourselves for the sake of others.

Boasting and Spiritual Experience (2 Cor 12:1–13)

Paul takes a new turn in the fool's speech in 12:1. Now he boasts, not of his sufferings, but of "visions and revelations of the Lord." We may assume once more that the opponents have forced Paul into boasting about this aspect of his life, for he only reluctantly introduces the topic. Because Paul says little about his private experiences in his letters, we know little about the role that they played in his life. We may assume that, despite his frequent visits and letters, the Corinthians also knew little about them. In Paul's speech before Agrippa in Acts, he describes the appearance of the risen Lord as a vision (Acts 26:19). In other instances he describes God's revelation as the driving force in his own life (Gal 1:12; 2:2) and a common experience in the life of the community (cf. 1 Cor 1:7; 14:6, 26). Here he speaks not of a singular vision or revelation but of "the exceptional character of the revelations" (12:7).

One particular event stands out in Paul's memory. He chooses not to speak of himself in 12:2–4, but of "a man in Christ" (12:2) or "such a person" (12:3) who "fourteen years ago was caught up into the third heaven." In Paul's time it was not uncommon to hear of someone being "raptured" into heaven. The apocalyptic writers speak of such events, as we may note from 2 En. 8:1: "And those men took me thence, and led me up to the third heaven, and placed me there in the midst of Paradise." The word "caught up" (ἁρπάζω) is used five times in the New Testament for those who are taken up into heaven (cf. Acts 8:39; 1 Thess 4:17a; Rev 12:5; 2 Cor 12:2, 3). Paul's experience was so overwhelming that he can date it "fourteen years ago." Although he speaks in the third person, he is obviously speaking of his own experience, as the first person in 12:1, 6–10 indicates. He chooses to speak in the third person because he refuses to boast personally of such experiences (12:5). Despite the power of the event, he has not told the Corinthians about it, for he does not want them to base their loyalty to him on anything other than what they see and hear in him (12:6). Although Paul obviously values such experiences, they do not constitute his credentials for ministry. Unlike the opponents, who apparently boast in their visionary experiences, he will boast only in his weaknesses (12:5).

The significance of Paul's ecstatic experience is suggested by the placement of the subject within Paul's argument: between the account of being let down in a basket (11:30–33) and the description of the thorn in the flesh in 12:7–10. Here Paul juxtaposes his ecstatic experience with another incident in his life that is otherwise unknown to us. The abundance of revelations might give him "an undue sense of his self-importance" (NRSV "in order to keep me from being too elated"), as it apparently had for the arrogant Corinthian opponents (cf. 11:20). Twice Paul uses this word to emphasize the problem of self-importance for those who boasted of their ecstatic experience (cf. 12:7). Consequently, Paul received the "thorn in the flesh," a chronic physical ailment in his life. We need not speculate on the nature of Paul's thorn in the flesh. The description of this messenger of Satan as something that "torments" (κολαφίζω) employs the image of striking with the fist, suggesting a continuing experience. We need only recall the Greek emphasis on physical health and stature and the opponents' charge that Paul's "bodily presence was weak." The Greeks highly esteemed physical qualities such as beauty, stature, agility, and health, and their contraries were made the subject of laughter and ridicule.[2] Greeks commonly compared themselves with others on the basis of birth, education, fertility, positions held, reputation, state of body, and general physical appearance.[3] The "thorn in the flesh" was probably the "weakness" for which Paul had been criticized.

According to 12:8–9 Paul prayed that the Lord would take the ailment away. "Three times" suggests especially intense prayer (cf. Matt. 26:44). Some have suggested that Paul's report of his prayers is actually a parody of ancient reports of prayers that brought the desired results. Paul indicates that God answered his prayer, but that God promised only the continuing grace to live in the presence of weakness. Paul's experience with the thorn in the flesh thus epitomizes his message to the opponents: that

2. Marshall, *Enmity at Corinth*, 153.
3. Marshall, *Enmity at Corinth*, 154.

power comes only in the context of weakness. Consequently, he concludes the fool's speech with a summary of the hardships that he has described already. He discovers the power of God in "weaknesses, hardships, persecutions, and calamities." He concludes appropriately, "When I am weak, then I am strong" (12:10).

In 12:11–13 Paul looks back over the fool's speech and summarizes its message. The Corinthians have forced Paul into foolishness by demanding his credentials (cf. 3:1–3) when they should have commended him themselves (cf. 11:1–16). He lacks nothing that the "super apostles" have (cf. 11:13, 18). Apparently, they claim "the signs of an apostle" (12:12), which Paul also possesses. He rarely mentions these signs and wonders (cf. Rom 15:18–19) but does so when the listeners have demanded it. The listeners have not been less favored than the other churches (cf. 11:7–11), for he has poured his life out for them.

Reflections for Preaching (2 Cor 12:1–13)

When we recognize that Paul's juxtaposition of his experiences of the ecstasy and agony of his ministry is a response to opponents who appealed to their experience to legitimize their ministry, we see our point of contact with the passage. Like the Corinthians, we recognize that our theology and our experience must ultimately meet. As Luke Timothy Johnson has pointed out,[4] many people, especially in the academic community, are more comfortable with doctrinal reflection than with the experience of power. On the other hand, popular religion expresses far more interest in religious experience than with theology. Indeed, many people, like the Corinthians, regard religious experience as the legitimating feature of their ministry.

Paul's juxtaposition of ecstasy and anguish may make everyone uncomfortable. On the one hand, he has a distinct place for religious experience. In his visions and revelations (12:1), his prayers (12:8–9), and "signs of an apostle," he recalls what he is reticent to tell: that religious experience is important for him. On the other hand, these experiences do not commend his ministry. Furthermore, his memory of "unanswered" prayer reflects the anguish of his faith.

Since 12:1–10 is a complete thought composed of the juxtaposition of two experiences, the sermon may reflect on the entire passage. In contexts in which religious experience plays a major role, the natural movement of

4. Johnson, *Religious Experience in Earliest Christianity.*

the passage allows us to place religious experience in perspective. We may begin with the affirmation of the importance of the "irrational" dimension of faith. In the sermon we may then examine the passage to see the ways in which Paul limits the focus on the experiential dimension of faith. We will observe (a) that such experiences do not legitimize our faithfulness (12:1–6) and (b) the fact that prayer does not bring automatic granting of our requests, but may result in the strengthening presence of God.

Final Visit, Final Argument (2 Cor 12:14—13:13)

Although Paul routinely mentions his future travel plans in his letters, only in 2 Corinthians does Paul weave his future travel plans throughout the final argument. Paul hinted at his plans in 10:2 before he launched into the climactic argument of the letter in 11:1—12:13. In 12:14 and 13:1 he mentions the impending visit once more, but the argument is not over. Between the references to the visit, he returns to the same themes that he has discussed throughout the letter, apparently hoping that one more argument will resolve the outstanding issues before he arrives. In 13:1–10 he returns to the theme of apostolic authority announced in 10:1–6, indicating that the next visit will not be like the last one, in which he was humiliated by some of the Corinthians. Paul prepares for the visit by stating his case a final time because he refuses to give up on this church that he has founded.

A Ministry for Others (2 Cor 12:14–21)

At the beginning of the letter, Paul stated that the aim of his ministry is that "on the day of the Lord Jesus we are your boast even as you are our boast" (1:14). As Paul anticipates his third visit, he expresses the concern that "I may find you not as I wish, and that you may find me not as you wish" (12:20). Despite the visits and the letters, Paul fears that his work with the Corinthians will be a failure—that he and the community will not live in the mutual admiration for which he had hoped. Instead of finding the Corinthians to be his "boast," he fears that God will "humble him" in the presence of this community (12:20). Consequently, Paul now reiterates his defense (12:14–15) against the charges that previously have been only implicit in the letter (12:16–18) and expresses his fears for the outcome of his work. Against the charge that he has taken advantage of them (12:16–18) for his own selfish reasons, he declares that his entire ministry has been for their sake (12:14–15, 19).

In 12:16–18 Paul now offers greater insight into the reasons he has defended himself throughout the letter. The Corinthians have accused Paul of being "crafty" (πανουγός) and acting with deceit (δόλος). They have also accused him of taking advantage of them, a charge that Paul also denied earlier in the letter (7:2). The charge that a teacher was interested only in the money was deeply rooted in ancient conversations among philosophers, who often accused their opponents of being greedy and deceitful. Paul answers the same suspicion in 1 Thess 2:5. The Corinthians were apparently saying, "He did not ask us for money for himself, but like a confidence trickster he used deceit to take us in. He could deny direct support from the Corinthians because he and his emissaries were taking the funds collected for Jerusalem." These charges in 12:16–18 provide the background for Paul's future demeanor on the upcoming visit.

Despite the suspicions, Paul says in 12:14–15 that he will not change his conduct. He has not burdened them in the past (11:9; 12:13), and he will not burden them in the future. In his statement "I do not want what is yours, but you," he expresses the fundamental principle of his ministry. Paul responded similarly to the gift from the Philippians: "Not that I seek the gift, but I seek the profit that accumulates to your account" (4:17). Paul had taught the Corinthians earlier not to "seek their own advantage" (10:24) and that "love does not insist on its own way" (13:5). In defending himself against suspicions in 2 Corinthians, Paul has insisted consistently that, in sharing the dying of Jesus (4:10), he no longer lives for himself (cf. 4:15).

Paul justifies his conduct with an appeal to nature, arguing that parents "lay up" (literally "treasure up") for their children rather than have children support their parents. Paul's illustration from parenthood was assumed in the ancient world. Aristotle, for example, indicated that the parent-child relationship has priority over all other relationships, describing it as an "unequal friendship" in which children can never repay parents' services but can respond only with love.[5] As a loving parent, Paul has the responsibility for his children. He disciplines them (1 Cor 4:14–21), is anxious for their upbringing (11:2), and provides for them. Indeed, on this final visit he will not only provide for them but "will spend and be spent" for them. The imagery of "spending" normally refers to the wasteful spending of money, as in the case of the prodigal son, who wasted everything (Luke 15:14). Here

5. Aristotle, *Eth. nic.* 8.7.2, quoted in Marshall, *Enmity at Corinth*, 247–51.

Paul speaks of spending himself to the point of exhaustion for the sake of the Corinthians. He employs a different metaphor to make the same point in Phil 2:17, when he describes himself as a sacrifice "poured out as a libation" for the sake of others. Paul makes the same point in 1 Thess 2:8 when he says, "we are determined to share with you not only the gospel of God but also our own selves, because you have become very dear to us." When Paul comes for a third visit, he will continue to show the same selflessness toward the Corinthians that he has shown in the past because he is an anxious father concerned for his children.

The goal of Paul's selfless activity, according to 12:19, is "to build you up." He had employed the imagery of the building in 1 Corinthians, declaring that he had laid the foundation to the building (1 Cor 3:10) and that others had built on to it. His greatest pastoral ambition was to ensure that the building survives until the end through the many tests that it will endure (1 Cor 3:10–17), and he instructs others to conduct themselves in order to build the community (cf. 1 Cor 8:1; 14:5). Here Paul explains that the building of the community is his ambition. He fears, nevertheless, that they will regress to their pre-Christian way of life. The vices that Paul lists in 12:20–21 are those of the Corinthians before their conversion ("impurity, sexual immorality, licentiousness"; cf. 1 Cor 6:9–11) or of the people while they were still in their infancy ("quarreling, jealousy, anger"; cf. 1 Cor 3:1–3). Paul fears that his pastoral ambition will not be fulfilled and that he will again grieve (cf. 2:1–4) when he comes to Corinth.

Reflections for Preaching (2 Cor 12:14–21)

Our point of entry is to find the central focus of 12:14–21 and to merge the horizon of the text with our own. When we treat this passage as a single unit, we see that Paul has come full circle from the thesis statement of 1:14. He fears that his selfless work on behalf of the Corinthians will not yield the results that he desires, but he has not abandoned his pastoral ambition. Despite his selfless love, the results are by no means assured. The focus of the passage, therefore, is its honest confession that our exhaustion for the sake of others does not guarantee the results that we desire. Despite the unpredictability of our results, discipleship involves our continued investment in service to others.

The sermon may begin with reflections on our assumption that hard work brings results. We know the success stories of those who have fulfilled their ambitions through determination and hard work. When it comes to working with people, we cannot always program the results, for we face numerous disappointments. Paul's model is a useful one for reflecting on our successes and failures as he continues to exhaust himself for others when he is unsure of the outcome.

"Examine Yourselves" (2 Cor 13:1–10)

The opening and closing words of chapters 10–13 form the "bookends" for Paul's concluding argument insofar as 13:1–10 largely repeats the themes of 10:1–11. In response to the charge that he was humble (= servile), he expressed the hope that when he was present he would not need to "show boldness by daring to oppose those who think we are acting according to human standards" (10:2). In 10:2, 8 Paul announces his authority, which he hopes not to use. Similarly, in 13:1–10 he announces his authority to punish but hopes not to need to use it. The Corinthian response to Paul's ministry—whether their continued resistance to Paul's teaching results in his humiliation (cf. 12:20–21)—will determine the outcome.

Paul describes his exercise of authority in the language of a trial (13:1), apparently using the procedures for a trial described in the Old Testament (Deut 19:15) as a metaphor for the action that Paul will take when he comes. He suggests that his three visits will fulfill the requirement for "three witnesses" and indicates that the next visit will not be like a previous occasion when he chose to "spare" the Corinthians (1:23); on this occasion he "will not spare" them. We do not know what procedure Paul has in mind—whether he is threatening to expel some from the church or promising some supernatural punishment. We do know that the Corinthians, who demand to see "proof" that Christ speaks through Paul, will now see the proof. The entire argument of 2 Corinthians suggests that the proof that the Corinthians seek is what they have not seen in Paul before, but have come to associate with the opponents: they want to see undeniable signs of power instead of the weakness that has distinguished his ministry. Perhaps having seen Paul's failure to show authority on his previous visit, they want to see a miraculous authority to punish wrongdoers. Paul responds, as he has throughout the letter, with the attempt to reshape their understanding of Christ, who "was crucified in weakness, but lives by the power of God" (13:4), and continues to "be weak in dealing with you, but is powerful in you" (13:3). In both Corinthian letters, Paul has shown that in the cross

God has inverted all of our values of strength and wisdom. Against ordinary human values, the theme of 2 Corinthians is that Paul's ministry is determined by the weakness of the cross. He comes in power, but not the power that the Corinthians expect.

In keeping with the focus of the entire letter on the legitimacy of Paul's ministry, the center of Paul's discussion in 13:1–10 is the "proof" (δοκιμή) of our ministry, as forms of δοκιμή are the threads running through this unit. In response to the Corinthians' demand for "proof" (13:3), he says in 13:5–10, "Examine yourselves to see whether you are in the faith. Test (δοκιμάζετε) yourselves." Then Paul speaks of the possibility that the Corinthians will "fail to meet the test" (13:6, be ἀδόκιμοι) or that he will "fail" (13:7, be ἀδόκιμοι). That is, after an entire letter in which Paul defends his ministry, he turns the tables in 13:5–10 to focus on whether those who are subjecting Paul to the test can pass the test themselves. What matters, as Paul concludes the letter, is not whether he has passed the test but whether they are restored to God. Paul offers a twofold prayer to indicate what really matters. In 13:7 he prays that they may do "what is right." In 13:9 he prays that they might become "perfect" (RSV "your improvement"). The latter word actually means "to be restored," or "put into proper condition." That is, Paul has not given up on this troublesome church. Despite their ingratitude to their spiritual father, he continues to pray for their complete restoration, hoping that he will never need to act severely, using the prophetic power that the Lord has given him.

Reflections for Preaching and Teaching (2 Cor 13:1–10)

The assembled community can find its hermeneutical orientation by identifying with the Corinthians. Having challenged Paul to give his credentials, they now face the test that will come with Paul's impending visit. The focus of the passage as well as the sermon is the challenge, "Examine yourselves to see whether you are living in the faith." The ultimate goal for the church, as Paul's prayers indicate, is to "do the good" (13:7) and to reach maturity (NRSV "perfection"). In the meantime we test ourselves to determine whether we are making progress or stand under condemnation. The criterion for measuring our progress is the extent to which we acknowledge the inversion of our values that the cross signifies.

God's Grace and Our Response (2 Cor 13:11–13)

Since 13:11–12 stands alone in the argument and includes Paul's standard exhortations (cf. Rom 15:5; Phil 2:2–5; 3:1; 4:4), we may wish to include this passage with the preceding one in order to offer examples of the community's role as it seeks to do the good. The lectionary's combination of the imperatives of 13:11–12 with the final benediction also offers a useful perspective for preaching, reflecting Paul's consistent insistence that the community is empowered by God's grace to conform to the expectations indicated in the imperative.

Paul commonly includes ethical exhortations that draw the consequences of his theological teachings near the end of his letters. In 2 Corinthians, however, he has said little about the concrete ethical demands of the Christian life until he comes to 13:11–12. These demands stand in contrast to the anti-social vices Paul fears that he will find in Corinth on his next visit (cf. 12:20). That is, despite the quarrels with the Corinthians, these demands indicate that he maintains hope for their future transformation. His ethical instructions are often a combination of generic qualities that he expects for all of his churches and characteristics that are especially at issue in specific letters. Undoubtedly, Paul introduced new converts to these communal norms at their conversion. The brief list here suggests that Paul is merely reminding the members of what they already know. When we recall that he addresses his instructions to the community that is gathered for worship, we recognize that Paul is attempting to build a cohesive moral community that has shared expectations and norms for conduct.

All of the imperatives suggest that Paul expects a rich community life for his converts. The opening imperative "rejoice" (NRSV "farewell" is a possible translation, but not the most likely) describes the conduct that Paul expects of all of his churches (cf. Phil 3:1; 4:4; 1 Thess 5:16). It is not to be trivialized into modern understandings of happiness but is rooted in the community's faith and hope (Rom 12:12). In the instruction to "put things in order" (καταρτίζεσθε), Paul employs the imagery of one who sets broken bones or mends nets (cf. Matt 4:21). He uses the noun form ("that you may become perfect") in 13:9. This command, which can be read either as the middle ("mend your ways" or "aim for restoration") or passive voice ("be restored"), suggests that the community is in need of a restoration, and that their participation in this process is vital. The phrase "listen to my appeal" (παρακαλεῖσθε) can also be translated "encourage one another." The exhortation to "agree with one another" is also a commonplace in Paul's exhortations (cf. Rom 15:5; Phil 2:2). Paul employs the ancient language of friendship that describes not those who agree on all points but those who are united in a common purpose. He assumes that the members of the community will, like other congregations, "live in peace" (cf. 1 Thess 5:13).

Paul adds one additional imperative that is common to all his letters. The command "Greet one another with a holy kiss" reflects the rich familial atmosphere of the early churches. Paul builds a family from people who come from a variety of social classes and ethnic groups. This consciousness of family extends beyond the house church, for Paul reminds the congregation that "all the saints greet you" (cf. Rom 16:16). As he plants churches throughout the empire, he creates an understanding that the local community has relationships in all of the distant places.

The distinctive feature of Paul's ethical teaching is that imperatives are accompanied by the promise of God's presence. That is, the community never stands alone to perfect itself but lives by the power of God. Paul ends the letter with the benediction that is similar to the conclusion of his other letters. In 13:11–13 he describes the one who will be *with* the community. In 13:11 his command for living in peace is followed by the promise that probably echoes the liturgy of the church: "The God of peace will be with you." In the benediction of 13:13, Paul expands on his usual benediction to give the trinitarian formula, which probably comes from the liturgy of the churches. His prayer for the "grace of the Lord Jesus Christ, the love of God, and the fellowship of the Holy Spirit" to be with the community is a reminder that the future well-being of the church rests not on its own abilities but on the resources that come from God.

Reflections for Preaching (2 Cor 13:11–13)

As the concluding word to a letter that is distinguished by tension and bitter irony, this passage places the struggles of church life in perspective. When we read this passage in context, the imperatives remind us of the shortcomings of the church and the need for its active participation in the work of building a loving community. In moving from the imperative to the indicative—from the demand to the promise—this passage offers a natural progression that can shape the movement of the sermon. In the first part of the sermon, we may focus on the fact that God calls us to be a model community that lives in harmony and peace—an impossible task. In the second part of the sermon, we find the assurances that God is present, equipping the church for its unfinished task.

BIBLIOGRAPHY

Amador, D. H. "Revisiting 2 Corinthians: Rhetoric and the Case for Unity." *New Testament Studies* 46 (2000) 92–111.

Beale, G. K. "The Old Testament Background of Reconciliation in 2 Corinthians 5–7 and its Bearing on the Literary Problem of 2 Corinthians 6.14–7:1." *NTS* 35 (1989) 558.

Danker, Frederick W. "Paul's Debt to the *De Corona* of Demosthenes: A Study of Rhetorical Techniques in Second Corinthians." In *Persuasive Artistry*, edited by Duane F. Watson, 262-80. Sheffield: Sheffield Academic Press, 1991.

Fant, Clyde. *Preaching for Today*. New York: Harper and Row, 1987.

Fitzgerald, John, *Cracks in an Earthen Vessel: An Examination of the Catalogues of Hardships in the Corinthian Correspondence*. Society of Biblical Literature Dissertation Series 99. Atlanta: Scholars, 1988.

Forbes, Christopher. "Comparison, Self-Praise and Irony: Paul's Boasting and the Conventions of Hellenistic Rhetoric." *New Testament Studies* 32 (1986) 1–30.

Hafemann, Scott. *Suffering and Ministry in the Spirit: Paul's Defense of his Ministry in II Cor 2:14–3:3*. Grand Rapids: Eerdmans, 1990

Johnson, Luke Timothy. *Religious Experience in Early Christianity: A Missing Dimension in New Testament Studies*. Minneapolis: Fortress, 1998.

Long, Fredrick J. *Ancient Rhetoric and Paul's Apology: The Compositional Unity of 2 Corinthians*. Society for New Testament Studies Monograph Series 131. Cambridge: Cambridge University Press, 2004.

Marshall, Peter. *Enmity at Corinth: Social Conventions in Paul's Relations with the Corinthians*. Wissenschaftliche Untersuchungen zum Neuen Testament. Tübingen: Mohr Siebeck, 1987.

Spicq, Ceslas. *Theological Lexicon of the New Testament*. Peabody, MA: Hendrickson, 1993.

Thompson, James W. "Reading the Letters as Narrative." In *Narrative Reading, Narrative Preaching*, edited by Joel B. Green and Michael Pasquarello III, 81–105. Grand Rapids: Baker Academic, 2003.

Webb, William. *Returning Home: New Covenant and Second Exodus as the Context for 2 Corinthians 6.14–7.1*. Journal for the Study of the New Testament Supplement Series 85. Sheffield: JSOT, 1993.

Windisch, Hans. *Der zweite Korintherbrief*. KEKNT. Göttingen: Vandenhoeck & Ruprecht, 1924.

Bibliography

Winter, Bruce W. *After Paul Left Corinth: The Influence of Secular Ethics and Social Change.* Grand Rapids: Eerdmans, 2001.

Witherington, Ben, III. *Conflict and Community in Corinth: A Socio-Rhetorical Commentary on 1 and 2 Corinthians.* Grand Rapids: Eerdmans, 1995.

Young, Frances, and David F. Ford. *Meaning and Truth in 2 Corinthians.* Grand Rapids: Eerdmans, 1988.